MID-LIFE

CYCLISTS

Chris McHutchison and Neil Blundell

ISBN 978-0-646-59093-6

To Mum and Dad

I gazed-and gazed-but little thought
what wealth the show to me had brought

William Wordsworth

Bicycle, bicycle, bicycle, bicycle, bicycle, bicycle

Anon

Contents

BEGINNINGS
(Chris)

I got passed by De Rosa. Well his name wasn't De Rosa, but he was a cyclist in a De Rosa jersey so I am going to call him that.

If you're a cyclist and another rider passes you, it hurts. It is not a mortal wound, for a middle-aged man in lycra, but it is a blow to the ego. When I got home, my wife asked how the ride was and all I could think about was the De Rosa pass. This was after ninety tough kilometres of cycling in the Hong Kong summer heat.

I summed up the whole ride with only three words.

'I got passed.'

The rest of the ride with its steep hills, angry dog, pot-holes, false flats, crazy bus drivers, hunger, thirst and fatigue was forgotten. All that mattered was the pass.

I was on the North Road around the airport in Hong Kong and was riding at about thirty kilometres per hour when De Rosa flew by in that nasty little cycling jersey covered in red hearts. Once passed of course I knew there was only one thing left to do, get back on his wheel.

I understand the rules of cycling. I know that cyclists can overtake you and you should accept that and move on. I know that sometimes you don't have the legs and your ego shouldn't get in the way and in my case I was out for a long, medium-paced ride and training for longer events. I should have let it slide. I get all that, but I had to catch him.

I clawed my way up to De Rosa's wheel with a few hard turns and sat there. I didn't want to yo-yo past, get caught again and be a pest, I just wanted to sit on his rear wheel and hang in there for a bit, as well as have a little break and prove I could be there if I wanted to. Still, he looked strong, and he had that lean muscled look of a genuine cyclist. Even in the blur of Rosa and hearts I could see his legs were shaved, unlike mine.

I tried to motor along behind him in near silence. No gear changes, no noise, no fuss. I didn't want him to know that I was there using him and his De Rosa shirt to hide from the wind. He did know though. All cyclists have a sixth sense when it comes to the wheel sucker.

We were fine for the first few kilometres, De Rosa and I the parasite, but the wind was coming from behind and he was reaching speeds of forty kilometres per hour. I was soon gasping. I had to change gears, and as I did I saw a slight turn of his head. He must have heard my cheaper components engage. I then started stamping on the pedals to keep up, grinding away and drawing in huge breaths, but alas, a tiny gap opened and within another kilometre or so he was gone. Off. Done. I gave up and watched the hearts grow smaller and buried the shameful episode away in my brain's cycling hits and memories section. I got passed by De Rosa.

My wife didn't understand at all of course and shook her head in response. She thinks it's more than a little childish to be upset at being passed, but that's how it is. I might be a forty year old weekend bike warrior of six feet two inches and eighty-eight kilograms who is not going to set any great records in the saddle but these incidents are of great consequence. I am a cyclist.

It was Neil Blundell who first introduced me to the sport. I was in London in 2001, an Aussie abroad, and working with Neil the Brit in the back office of a bank in Lower Thames Street. We had zero work to do, day after day. My reporting line was to Neil, who was a few years younger than I, and I was doing little more than cutting and pasting data on a spreadsheet for a very respectable twenty pounds per hour. A couple of times I mentioned to Neil that I was running out of things to do and wondered why I was hired. He laughed and told me to keep quiet and just 'get on with it'. I wasn't sure what I was to get on with but in the end I got the message and managed to make it look like I was struggling to get through the ton of work I pretended to have.

As a result we had plenty of time to share stories and especially those about cycling. Neil told me one day about an Etape he had ridden. This was a stage of the Tour de France he said, and added that I might have heard of it, even in Australia. At the time I thought riding an Etape made him a semi-professional, an athlete on the cusp of breaking into the professional ranks. He said that this Etape was held the day before the pro riders. I ventured aloud whether it was a sort of trial to see if there were any semi-pros who could be offered a contract. Neil let me believe this falsehood for some time.

Neil likes to talk, and he peppers his conversation with words and phrases that I now understand but had little clue about at the time. I was an Australian in England and fresh off the boat, but I had heard some cockney slang and London lingo over the years and thought I could handle myself in the bars of the city. It was a steep learning curve with Neil though. For instance when I mentioned one of the girls in the office was pretty; Neil told me she had a 'dodgy boat'. I think I stared at him and blinked. Apparently a boat is a face, because 'boat race' rhymes with face, almost, and having a dodgy boat meant having a dodgy face. No, it can't be adequately explained.

I then asked him about the pub we were going to that night. He said it was 'pony'. That brought about more staring and blinking. I won't go into it in detail but 'pony and trap' rhymes with crap. He was trying to tell me the pub was crap.

Neil's jargon extended to cycling but there was less of the rhyming slang at least. There was talk of back doors being blown off, big dogs, big rings, getting dropped, granny gears, back cogs, the hog, the bonk, a man with a hammer, you name it.

Various riders were, according to Neil, 'on the PEDs'. He didn't hold back with his opinions on current and former pros. He was a fan of guys like Pantani, Indurain, and Boogerd and of course the Briton, Chris Boardman, while he voiced doubts and dispensed nasty comments about others such as Lance. I should say that Neil did convince me to keep an eye on Cadel Evans, even way back in 2003. He said that Cadel couldn't be 'on the PEDs' because he looked too grim when he was riding. He told me Cadel was permanently 'on the rivet', always looked like he was 'about to explode' and that's what he liked about him.

Later Neil showed me an article he had written about the Etape event for a cycling magazine detailing his own completion of the stage, all one hundred and forty nine kilometres and four alpine climbs of it, including a section where his mate was swept up into something called a broom wagon. On reading the article I gathered this Etape was for people of all shapes and sizes though Neil certainly looked like an athlete, being lean and without an ounce of fat.

In terms of a cycling career, Neil had ridden local amateur races in his county of Kent with reasonable results but never made it to the next level. Competition is tough in England and only the top one or two stars from a pool of thousands in each county can expect to make the transition so this is no shame. What Neil lacks in athletic ability however he makes up for in buying prowess. The man is a bike retailer's dream. Not a week goes by where he hasn't made some sort of purchase whether it is a top of the range pair of sunglasses or a simple brake pad. He is a giant of internet shopping in particular, constantly putting the web browsing miles in and is an avid believer in quality and expense, with the emphasis on expense. Neil's mantra is 'you have to buy the best, to look the best, to be the best' and he lives up to this. It is a chant I would hear many times in the coming years.

My own bond with cycling was soon formed. I was hooked on the sport as a spectacle, with the tours and the classics soon providing countless hours of viewing and reading entertainment. A bond with Neil was also formed. Despite moving back to Australia we emailed daily about the pros, upcoming events, new kit and new books, and eventually my own physical entry into the world of cycling.

Neil was the first of three catalysts for my love of cycling. At this point cycling for me was still only a spectator sport. It seemed like a good way to work off the few pounds that had joined me in recent years but I wasn't yet read to get out on the road.

I had no interest in participating. Many of my Australian friends joked about lycra-clad skinny cyclists embarrassing themselves in garish outfits while sipping lattes; it is not seen as a manly pursuit. An additional negative, one seemingly in conflict with that perception of unmanliness, is that it can be a dangerous sport.

I was in my early thirties and no longer participating in any sport at all apart from surfing. While I was still in reasonable shape, the years were starting to creep around my belly like the rings on a tree, increasing with age. I needed a push in the direction of the saddle and this was soon to come.

THE BELGIAN CONNECTION
(Chris)

The history of cycling is full of stories of professional cyclists taking up riding on a whim or a recommendation from someone already inside the sport. Richie Porte, pink jersey wearer in the Giro D'Italia, was a triathlete, as was Lance Armstrong. Another Australian, Simon Gerrans, winner of Milan San-Remo and a Tour de France stage, raced motorbikes. He credits his neighbour with encouraging him to ride bicycles after he had suffered a crash by suggesting it would aid recovery. The neighbour, Phil Anderson, was himself a Tour De France stage winner and the first Australian to wear a yellow jersey, hence his somewhat biased advice that cycling would be of medical benefit. I needed my own Phil Anderson to get me out there on the road.

In 2006 my Phil Anderson did appear, in the form of a beautiful Belgian, Wendy, who eventually became my wife. I should say that Wendy is much better looking than Phil. She is stunning, and scores far better than Phil in terms of aesthetics. Thinking about it now though, Phil Anderson has worn the yellow jersey so perhaps points should be deducted from Wendy. Actually, truth be known, I could be leaning in the direction of Phil if it ever came down to a choice...but I'm straying from the issue.

Essentially Wendy and her provenance are the real reasons for my love of bikes. She is Belgian, more specifically Flemish, and hails from the town of Essen which sits way up in the north-east of Flanders. Essen is the last train stop before Roosendaal in Holland. Much Dutch culture made it through to the normally guarded Flemish people in this part of the country including the use of Dutch salutations and a passion for liquorice or 'droppekes'. Essen used to be as bustling as any small village can be in Belgium, particularly in its former life as a customs port. When the European Union pulled down borders, business in Essen fell away and the town developed a sleepy, restful aspect which continues to this day.

Belgians love bikes. For starters it is easy to ride in Belgium as much of the country is dead flat. The area is known in Flemish (or Dutch) as the 'Lage Landen'. The first word is pronounced like the English word 'lager' but the name doesn't have anything to do with Belgium's renowned expertise in lager. Instead 'Lage' can be translated as *low* and 'landen as *lands* i.e. *the low-lands*. Those who named it were spot on. The only hill within one hundred kilometres of Essen is a ramp into the small shopping centre car park. There is also not much in the way of high rise buildings, so from your bicycle you can see mile after mile of plains and farmlands, with the odd church spire or bridge in the distance.

Belgium in terms of bikes is a Dr. Seuss story. Big, small, fat, tall, long, short, old, new, you can't see the country for bikes. My father-in-law has five. One for the road in good weather, one for the road in bad, one for the woods, one for the shops, one spare. My mother-in-law has four. These include bikes for the kids that have grown up and moved away, a bike for visitors and a bike for spare parts. Looking in the garage I'm sure the bikes had gotten together and made baby bikes. There are trikes; there are three-seater bikes, there are bikes with baskets and bikes with caskets.

I had no option but to join. Off to the shops, get on your bike. Off to Tante Ria, get on your bike. Off to the station, get on your bike. We went to a fair in the middle of a cornfield somewhere and took our bikes. When we got there we dropped the bikes in to a sort of 'bike paddock' at rest alongside thousands of other bikes. I started taking photos of the bikes while laughing and asked how on earth we would be able to remember where we left ours given the mass of others in similar colour, shape and style, all leaning against each other. Wendy wasn't sure what the problem was and gave me a strange look. A friend of hers overheard this and said that if we couldn't find ours we could just take someone else's. Nice.

I also slowly started getting used to seeing men in lycra up close and personal rather than from the safety of a car, or on television. Wendy's father, Lucien, is in a local fiets (bike) club in Essen called ''t Pedalleke'. The little pedal. He retired from service on the Belgian trains at the age of fifty-five and is spending his retirement in the saddle. Lucien rides at least three days a week, and clocks up ten thousand kilometres every year with each ride recorded in a notebook. Most of the rides are club rides, including a seventy kilometre club ride every weekend, but he also rides on his own and often completes longer round trips of one hundred and fifty to two hundred kilometres with a smaller group of three or four friends. He has won the yellow jersey of the 't Pedalleke cycling club classic in Essen for the last three years. This event is not just about the race, it's also about the bike. You have to change a tyre tube as part of the course. Epic.

Additionally, Lucien doesn't do maps. This is a man who would eventually take me for a ride from his house in Essen all the way through beautiful Belgium and Holland to the Zeelandbrug and back, at around one hundred and sixty kilometres in total, without ever once looking at a map or a signpost or even the direction of the sun. We went over bridges and across valleys, down back lanes and through village squares. We went over railway crossings, and past windmills, tulip farms and corn fields all the time like he was popping down the driveway to his own letterbox. The man knows his cycling routes.

The first sight of Lucien the lycra man over my breakfast coffee and eggs, was mildly disconcerting. In fact let me make a correction there; it was extremely alarming. It has taken me years to get used to the body hugging and stretching effects of lycra. The alarm bells don't ring any more, at least not as loudly, but no-one needs to see that in the morning. Admittedly he is in great shape. Cycling has kept the pounds off, and he hasn't even a wisp of hair on his legs. Yes I know, I've looked closely, and I've spent countless hours staring at those legs while on a bike in the back of the bunch trying to hang on. They look like thin, brown, smooth table legs with cycling shoes planted at the bottom. Added to this, for the enjoyment of my first lycra breakfast, was the stark contrast between the hairless legs of Lucien and his arms, which are of the silverback gorilla variety. There is a lot of hair on those arms and indeed a lot of hair also bursts through the top of his cycling jersey. He is very lucky with his cycling legs though. He tells me, in fact he tells everyone, that he has never had hair on his legs, not once, and has *never* shaved them. It is just some sort of miracle. I'm going to leave it there.

I should thank Lucien, profusely, for raising his daughter with a deep understanding of the need for men to be on bikes for hours. There can be no end of thanks for this. Wendy says that he rode every Sunday morning without fail. There are other days of course but Sunday morning is the dedicated morning of the ride where nothing else can take precedence. According to my wife, ever since she was a toddler, and probably way before, he would be out at eight and back no earlier than one. And this is the great bit for me: my wife thinks this is perfectly normal. *Of course you should be out with your mates on a bike every Sunday. Why not take Saturday too? Three bikes? But don't you need four? And an indoor trainer? My Dad has those roller thingies too, maybe you should try those.*

Thank you, Belgium.

I can only imagine how different it would be to have a wife brought up in an environment where cycling is viewed as a ridiculous pastime for mid-life crisis desperados. I have never once come home to an upset wife in hair curlers slapping her palm with a rolling pin wondering where I have been. Again, thank you.

I try not to take Wendy's good grace for granted and never use all my permitted hours. I even ignore her comments when I drag myself back home after a hard ride and she tells me I've aged ten years in two hours. Thanks for that, too.

This, let's call it *love* of cycling by Wendy also extends to our home television viewing. Often she will turn the channel to Sporza or Eurosport without my prompting, even if it is for Ghent-Wevelgem, or the Tour of Turkey, when we really should be doing something else. Basically my wife is as comfortable with cycling on in the background as the average Australian lady finds herself with cricket. I should add that I am still working on the cricket piece.

Wendy also had a brush with cycling fame in her wilder days. At a night club in Belgium she was dancing away with her best friend and looked up to see Tom Boonen standing in front of her. Tom Boonen is the most famous of all current Belgian cyclists, an absolute superstar.

'Hi, Wendy,' Tom said, beaming at her.

Wendy's eyes opened wide in shock and she put her hand to her chest.

'Oh my God! Tom Boonen, how do you know my name?'

'Well…..you are wearing a necklace with 'Wendy' spelt out in massive letters.'

Shock turned to disappointment, and then laughter. Ultimately her pride was intact. It didn't matter whether a sparkling 'Wendy' necklace had been the prompt for their short dialogue, the king of Belgium had spoken to her.

Equally as enamoured with cycling is Wendy's grandmother. Moemoe, as she is affectionately known, is eighty-three and lives in a small white cottage in Essen with one of her sons. The walls inside are like most grandmother's houses and are decorated with photographs of loved ones taken recently and in days gone by. There's the wedding day of each of her daughters, photographs of Wendy as a baby, photographs of cheeky cousins and old portraits of Moemoe's husband. This is where the comparison to a non-Belgian house ends however because the largest photo of all, dwarfing the others at almost poster size, is of Moemoe standing next to Tom Boonen. It is a full length shot. He is in Quick Step team cycling gear clutching a bunch of flowers with his arm around Moemoe, beaming those massive Belgian pearly whites of his.

There are still no photos of me on the wall, either in or out of cycling kit, despite countless visits to the house, many while bearing gifts, even after five years of marriage to her granddaughter. I have a photo of myself in Assos jersey and bib shorts I've been meaning to send, but I am not sure it would make the cut.

Less surprising is the Belgian media's devotion to cycling. The newspaper dedicates most of its sports section to Wielrennen before permitting a few column inches of the ho-hum world game of football for instance. When the Tour de France is on there is a daily lift-out section of about ten pages and every evening on television there is a one hour package of Tour highlights and discussion at prime time. Lifestyle and celebrity magazines, even outside the regular summer cycling season, are filled with interviews with Phillipe Gilbert, Jurgen Van Den Broeck and Robbie McEwen.

When I say summer season, I should clarify. Unlike many cycling nations there is a very real winter cycling season in Belgium which is hugely popular. The riders participate in one-day events known as cyclocross which are huge affairs held in a different province every weekend. Thousands of Belgians spend their wintry Saturday and Sunday afternoons on small, muddy, freezing fields in Flanders watching riders complete up to nine laps of a circuit in an hour or so. The course cannot usually be ridden completely on the saddle due to stretches of mud, sand, puddles and snow. Short, steep climbs dotted around the trail are also on hand, forcing riders to dismount and stagger up on foot while carrying bikes on their shoulders. These athletes are super-fit and the top ten each year will earn a comfortable living and considerable fame from the sport.

The crowds love it too, some even preferring cyclocross to the road racing of the Pro Tour. Those attending arrive early and spend the whole day watching the junior, women's and pro events while eating fries and burgers, washed down with beer after beer after beer, served mostly in plastic cups. There is often trouble and fighting amongst partisan crowds cheering on particular riders from home provinces. Marshalls fight valiantly to hold back beer-soaked fans roaring into the cyclist's ears as they ride past in the tight circuits. These cyclists wryly complain later they can determine the type of beer from the breath of the spectators. At around four, as the early winter nights descend, the drunken scene resembles Woodstock, though the muddied Flemish crowds are swaying individually and out of time rather than collectively, and are paying homage to cyclists rather than Hendrix.

My brother-in-law is a policeman and now schedules a day of annual leave when the cyclocross is in town. He does not want to be anywhere close to that mess. Two years ago he went home and found a tooth stuck in the sole of his boot. He must have trodden on it after a brawl. Last year he was in the front of his police car with a colleague when they saw a portable toilet being moved by two drunks, from a field, onto the middle of a road. The two policemen sighed, got out of their vehicle, walked over to the pranksters and asked for the toilet to be put back. Suddenly they heard a horn. Turning around they saw that another drunk had crawled into the front seat of their police car and was honking, waving and laughing. They returned to the car, took his beer, arrested him and locked him in the back. On doing this however they were pelted by snowballs from yet another swarm of intoxicated Belgians. They jumped into the front seats. A security guard defied the incoming snowballs and tapped on the side of the police car in order to tell Wendy's brother that the man in the back was wanted for an earlier assault. It was a lucky arrest. On their way to the police station they drove slowly passed two men preparing to fight. One of the men delicately removed his front teeth and placed them in his top pocket, with a pat for safe keeping, before raising his fists.

In a cyclocross event in December 2012, Sven Nys (world champion in February 2013), had fallen twice and was in the middle of the pack, out of the running. A young spectator threw the contents of a cup of beer over him as he rode past. Sven Nys got off his bike and chased the offender, a seventeen-year-old boy, across a field and remonstrated with him. He later told the media that he is not an animal and does not deserve to be covered in beer. Many were unimpressed, suggesting he only got off his bike because he was losing.

Cycling is everything in Belgium. There is a constant swarm of bikes in and around Belgian villages, towns and cities with people buying bread, travelling to work, visiting friends and out training on an incalculable variety of two wheeled steeds. Cycling is not just a way of life in Belgium; it is almost the only way of life.

ETAPE DU TOUR
(Neil)

I haven't always been fanatical about cycling, that came later, probably sometime around 1998 after I had immersed myself in a few other sports and unceremoniously jacked them all in. After a few years of riding around the villages of Kent I felt I needed to test myself with a new challenge, and not just any challenge, but something that would push me physically and mentally to the limit. A work colleague, Richard, who was an encyclopedia of all things sport and had a huge interest in the Tour De France suggested I try the Etape. The Etape is a one day cycling event held on the rest day of the Tour and is open to any cyclist of any ability to enter. It is usually raced in mid-July and encompasses a mountain stage featuring various monuments, or famous mountains, from Le Tour. The organisers close off all of the roads and provide food and support to the entrants. In short, you are treated like a professional. Unfortunately they also provide a humiliating broom wagon to sweep up the also-rans who don't make set cut-off times along the way. Richard also suggested that he would come along which was a surprise given he had almost never mentioned cycling before. I was a little unsure of how I would be able to complete such a challenge, especially having only ridden the odd one-kilometre climb around Kent. Richard was an altogether different proposition. Once the gauntlet was thrown down and my courage questioned I wasn't able to say no. The stage was set. Now all I had to do was prepare.

The first thing I did was buy more kit. You can never have enough. Well at least I can never have enough. The age old maxim of needing n+1 bikes, with n being the number you currently have is different for me. In terms of kit for instance, be it jerseys, socks, creams, shorts, jackets, warmers, or sunglasses I need n *squared*. That is also what I told Laura who noticed various packages arrive in a flurry. You have to buy the best in order to look the best before you can be the best.

The kit buying process was far and away the most enjoyable part of tackling the Etape. That insignificant other known as training had also started off quite well and went from November through to the beginning of February. Some appalling English weather had failed to give me even a hint of a cold and I had ridden at least three times a week on various hilly and flat low intensity rides.

I soon booked two weeks holiday in France and was riding up to four hours every second day. Riding a bike on the road in Britain is not always a pleasurable experience, especially in the era prior to Team GB's phenomenal Olympic success, and I can remember countless occasions of being cut up on the road and threatened with many fascinating forms of usually incoherent but always unmistakable violence. France took this to the next level however.

On one particular instance a driver decided that he, his Renault, and his passengers absolutely had to knock me down at all costs. I was behind him at the time but this was no great obstacle for he soon put his car in reverse and came straight back at me. This required some quick thinking on my part and an even quicker vault of a thicket fence in order to avoid being flattened like a crepe. Luckily I had somehow managed to push the bike in a separate direction. Two men and a 'lady' then began screaming French abuse out of the windows and over the top of each other for about a minute before deciding my lack of response meant I was an imbecile and they drove off, still shouting. This French auto-entertainment was almost as interesting as the countryside.

Richard on the other hand conceived his own local method of training which was to restrict his drinking to only ten pints twice a week rather than his usual tally, and walking to the Raj Rani Curry House instead of ordering home delivery. Additionally he had completed 'about four weeks of exercise bike work in the gym' whatever that entailed, and had been out on the road with me twice. In his US Postal gear he cut a sturdy figure, reminding me of a rugby player rather than a well-honed endurance athlete.

Of the two rides that we did complete together, I say *together* in the loosest sense of the word, a few warning signs were becoming apparent. Richard told me that he was a big gear man. He liked to 'feel the gear' and his muscles working hard. High cadence was not for him. Richard was an expert in the matter and would not heed any advice.

His big gear theory was thoroughly evident on our first ride together as he mashed his pedals at about sixty revolutions per minute on the flat. When the first hill loomed into view he told me that he would use the gear to power up the climb. His cadence dropped to about forty however as he point blank refused to get out of the big ring. We, in turn, were getting slower and slower and I wondered at his cycling prowess. Was he perhaps lulling me into a false sense of security? I decided to test the theory by sprinting up the hill. I didn't turn back until the top as I thought it may have been fatal if he hurtled around me. Needless to say he wasn't there. When he eventually reached the top he mumbled something about 'getting on the juice.'

The second ride was much longer with more climbs, some of which were fairly vicious eighteen percent beasts and really sapped the energy. It was on this ride that Richard decided that completing the Etape would probably be too much for him, but he was going to give it a go anyway. Chapeau.

My confidence was high, perhaps a little too high as the training started to wind down into taper mode many months out from the July Etape. I almost stopped buying kit too. By April my motivation was on the wane. Training was playing havoc with my social life. Laura was becoming increasingly irate with me getting up at ridiculous times in the morning to 'get the miles in'. A few weeks out from the event though the realization set in that I was about to tackle famed beasts of the French Alps with a significant lack of fitness. Looking the best to be the best seemed now to be ninety-nine percent of my makeup.

By mid-June, with the Etape only weeks away I attempted to force fit myself which is like force feeding but with huge training rather than eating. Instead of new thighs and a six pack I developed knee problems and a bad back. Spirits were flagging. Then came the French glazed cherry on top; a crash.

I had a nasty collision with an absent-minded tri-athlete which was most definitely not the fault of my own masterly bike handling skills. He piled into me at an intersection and I found myself facing repair bills of slightly less than five hundred pounds as well as several remedial trips to the bike shop. The bike shop visits were a positive I hasten to add.

As you can tell, the excuses were mounting up on the bike more than I was. As I didn't hold a racing licence I would also require a letter from my general practitioner confirming that there was a fairly low probability I would end up on a mortuary slab if I competed in the Etape. The examination itself was not the most thorough medical I have endured. The doctor was a locum, which probably explains the indifference, and simply held a stethoscope to my chest to confirm that I was indeed in possession of a beating heart. The letter was duly signed and I was good to go.

With this knowledge I set about packing my extensive bike gear and most importantly, the bike itself. I hired a cycle box from Geoffrey Butler cycles which promised to take the worry out of transporting my precious bike on the plane. Packing it was simple enough, re-assembling the bike when I finally got to France was going to be a challenge.

With the bike eventually packed and the life insurance signed (Laura wanted the car and stereo apparently) I set off to Heathrow with Richard.

On the outbound flight out we met two fellow cyclists who, to use their own words, had not 'done much training... but we do the odd triathlon'. We soon learned that they had participated in the Hawaii ironman with one completing it, and they had both reconnoitered the whole Etape route in addition to climbing the final mountain 'in both directions.' By the end of the flight we realised that our own preparations on the flats of Kent were woefully inadequate and we were going to get our butts kicked.

After a long coach trip from the airport we arrived at the bottom of Les Arcs, scene of the first chinks being exposed in Big Mig's armour in the 1996 Tour De France. Richard and I proceeded to turn white as the mountain ramped up with hairpin bend after hairpin bend. Richard proposed taking the next flight home with a straight face, and then suggested we instead sprint to the front of the race like men possessed before crashing out spectacularly. We could then tell everyone we would have won but for a patch of oil.

Once we were happily settled in at the top of Les Arcs, we set about re-assembling our bikes which was difficult for someone with my bike maintenance skills and took three hours. We then shortly enjoyed some fine French cuisine and proceeded down to a local bar for a few beers. It was fantastic pre-ride preparation.

After possibly the worst night sleep of my life, due to thinking about the torture ahead, we trundled down to breakfast only to be told that we would have to ride down to the start village and ride back. Riding down to the start village didn't really bother me until the first drops of rain appeared at the window, but riding eighteen kilometres up an Hors Category or 'so steep it can't be categorised' climb, with an average gradient of seven percent, the day before the stage, sounded like French lunacy.

The descent from Les Arcs in the torrents of rain was quite amusing especially as the French had neglected to tell us that they were digging huge holes in the road. This really didn't go well with twenty pairs of expensive Mavic wheels and bikes swerved violently across the road to avoid the wounded tarmac. Once at the start village we collected our race numbers and took refuge from the rain in a little pub with a mug of horlicks. Richard had already decided he didn't want to ride the thirty kilometres back to the hotel so we set about trying to find the easiest and more importantly, flattest route back. As luck would have it we rode into, literally on Richard's fatigued part, an old guy and his wife who were walking up the mountain on a whim. They took us to a very handy ski lift which sent us virtually to the top with only two kilometres or so to ride ourselves. Merci beaucoup!

We met some other guys from our party at the summit who had the same idea as us and chatted about various cycling related topics before finding a route to the hotel. We all got hopelessly lost. I decided to have a quick pit stop with Richard when suddenly the route was found and a mini race began up Les Arcs. I started about thirty metres behind everyone so had to sprint up by which time the group had exploded, quite literally in fact. The rear derailleur from one Briton had decided now was time to spontaneously shatter onto the road bringing him to a complete stop and a frantic few hours travelling around town to get it fixed. The mini burn up continued, there were only two riders ahead of me, I decided to test the legs and move up. This was the first physical shock of the trip as I was really struggling for air. By the time I reached them my breathing was all over the place.

I tried to show my fellow riders that I wasn't even out of breath but once out of view I collapsed on the floor in a sweaty heap.

The holiday Etape literature proclaimed that on the night before the race we were to be given a pasta party with huge volumes of pasta and rice to aid us in our quest for glory.

We spruced ourselves up for this 'carbo disco' but were to be sorely disappointed. The organiser had neglected to tell the hotel of our high carbohydrate needs and we were instead served salad and a sorry piece of salmon that looked like it had been fasting in the sun. I hate fish.

We left the restaurant and returned to our rooms in poor spirits, with hungry bellies. Three chocolate bars and a sports drink soon fixed that and we started to feel better. I attached my race number to the jersey and settled down for a second fitful night of sleep, in part due to the sugar rush.

At four thirty am we were woken by my alarm. Richard rolled out of bed and had his first of many 'toilet' stops. When Richard came back into the room I was in the middle of changing. He proclaimed that I looked like someone with an eating disorder which managed to be both offensive and vaguely satisfying. I told him he looked like an overweight darts player which I guess was neither.

We went down for a breakfast which carried over the previous evening's theme of sending riders off on a mountain stage half-starved. Either the French had not heard of eating the best to be the best or they were concerned by the arrival of the portly English and American hordes and took matters in hand.

The coach left at five forty-five am with one poor guy being forced to cycle down to the start because the driver couldn't fit his bike on the van that was following us. The bus was deadly silent apart from the odd charmer passing wind.

When we finally reached Aime, Richard yet again decided that 'a big poo' would lighten the load on his bike. Perhaps he was the charmer on the bus. He started to queue for a crowded toilet that I understand made the loo from the film *Trainspotting* look like the Queen's private throne.

We were pencilled in to begin the race at the three thousand people to five thousand people section but because of the impromptu toilet stops we were positioned right at the very back. By this point I had already decided that my goals were:

a) To finish, and

b) Not to stop on the climbs, and

c) Slit my wrists if Richard beat me.

The announcer read out the names of the race favourites; Christophe Rinero, Tour De France King of the Mountain in 1998, Jerome Chiotti and Alain Prost. My name was not part of this list.

A starter's gun fired in the distance to signal that we were underway. The butterflies in my stomach burst into life. It took ten more minutes until the crowds had moved sufficiently for me to turn the pedals however.

I shook hands with Richard and took a photo. Little did I know I wouldn't see him for another eight hours.

The pace at the start was pretty slow with most people content to have a bit of a chat and roll along. After about ten minutes I had an incredible urge to go to the bathroom which was to be the first of many toilet stops. The route map showed the first thirteen kilometres to be slightly uphill but it hardly felt it as we cruised along. Many obviously worried about the first mountain, the nineteen kilometre long brutal Cormet de Roselend. We piled through the village and turned a quick corner and there it was. A huge group of riders were at the base of the col and were unfortunately travelling at roughly two miles per hour. The skill on show was immense as every rider wobbled sluggishly along whilst endeavouring to stay clipped into the pedals. It would have been faster to walk, backwards.

This was to be a feature of the early part of the Roselend: slow progress followed by riders coming to a complete standstill and extreme, low speed crashes. Eventually we started to get moving but the progress was painfully slow and after four very nervous kilometres we turned up a hairpin and everything stopped for a few hundred metres. People were walking and we couldn't see why. We dismounted, as riding was near impossible, and trudged up the mountain in clippetty cloppetty cleats. I looked to my right to see a young lady leaking tears by the side of the road.

Finally the field started to clear and we managed to get going again. It was at this point that a yellow flash out of the corner of my eye caught my attention. A yellow jersey in full US Postal kit with a top of the range Trek bike sprinted past the field out the saddle, Lance style. This raised a few wry smiles from the wily old French and Belgian campaigners. I would meet this guy again further up the road, but more of that later.

The road was still pretty packed and the pace fairly slow but this gave me a chance to admire the superb views across the valleys. It was truly a cycling paradise like no other. Further up the field was thinning and this was when I had my first nasty shock of the day, a sign saying fifteen kilometres to go. This is when reality set in. I was not here for the vistas. I was in 39x25 and pedalling quite easily. A nasty section of hairpins and steep sections confronted us so I changed down to my bottom gear of 39x27 and tried to 'spin' it. I came to the conclusion that if I wanted to save my legs, for what I never did find out, I would push low gears at all times and keep well within myself.

Back down the road Richard was having problems of his own. After deciding to keep his rain jacket on at the start he now had no opportunity to take it off. As he was steadily cooking in his jacket, he needed to replenish the fluids regularly and at one point promptly dropped his bottle to shouts of 'Sacre bleu!' He followed my earlier advice of 'do not *ever* get off' and sadly watched the bottle roll off the mountain. With only one water bottle, temperatures rising, and carrying his solid torso to the sky he was going to be in real trouble.

I, on the other hand, was having a better time and decided these low gears were rather brilliant. I was spinning away quite happily, avoiding various objects strewn all over the road. There were Oakleys, at least four pairs, and pumps galore. I got to the front of a small group going fairly sedately and upped the pace a tad. A few guys just kept on my wheel for the next mile or so. I then put in an old style Virenque attack, out the saddle for about twenty seconds and came up to another group. My legs then emphatically let me know that 'we won't be doing that again' so for the rest of the climb I rode at my own boring and metronomic pace.

The last three kilometres toward the peak seemed to just drag on and on. The temperature was cooling and the wind increasing and the spectacular view of Mont Blanc had riders gasping for reasons of both beauty and want of oxygen.

The sight of the feeding station at the top of the climb was another welcome view. The feeding station resembled a wild chaotic free for all. It was a stampede for water, cake, bananas and deliciously sun-warmed ham and cheese sandwiches. At first I didn't enter the scrum, thinking that it would all calm down in a minute or two. Five minutes later nothing had changed so I waded in and started scoffing.

After spending about fifteen minutes munching bananas and taking on too much water, I pulled up the arm warmers. Bizarrely I had also been wearing knee warmers for the duration of the event despite temperatures reaching thirty-two degrees Celsius, but these were great for the descent and I took off down the mountain.

I had never cycled down an Alpine descent before and the whole experience was really quite unnerving at first, especially with the maniac Frenchies passing at ridiculous points and frightening speeds. By now I was wishing I had put a jacket on, as the knee warmers were not enough. My whole body was shivering and shaking. I also hit a nasty bump which jarred my neck and meant I could no longer use the drop handlebars without pain.

When I eventually reached the bottom I stopped to have another pit stop. We cruised through the town. A nice set of cobbled speed bumps gave me a wedgie and reminded me there were other cycling hazards aside from mountain climbs.

The crowds in the town, yes there were crowds lining the roads for me, were giving us a few cheers and I thought to myself 'this isn't so bad. Look at me, I'm an athlete.' The next Col would change my mind completely.

The Col de Saises loomed large. There was a hairpin right and then the fifteen kilometre climb started in earnest. On paper this appeared to be the hardest climb and regrettably the route plan was correct, it was a monster. The gradient, whilst not being a complete killer, was relentless. There were seemingly no breaks at all in the climb. The mid afternoon heat, made worse under our helmets, was starting to tell on the blotchy red faces of the riders around me and I dare say my own.

Nevertheless, heat and gradient were not the only worries. I started to get a gnawing pain in my stomach which gradually grew worse and worse. Combined with an urge to go to the bathroom again I really needed to stop and sort myself out. I had set a goal of no stopping on the climbs for whatever reason, and that was the way it was going to be.

Riders were dropping like flies on the climb. The combined gradient and heat cut them down one by one and they cut lone figures on the roadside, exhausted and beaten. A flash of yellow caught my eye again. I turned my head to the left and saw the crumpled figure of the Lance Armstrong wannabe, vomiting next to his bike. That was the last of him.

The ride was turning into a battle of wills and I forced myself to carry on plodding up the road at a low cadence, with stomach cramps worsening. By the time I reached the top of the climb I really didn't feel good at all. I decided to stuff myself with anything I could lay my hands on at the feed station: stale sandwiches, bananas, oranges and biscuits until I started to feel a bit sick. I vaguely calculated that by the time I reached the foot of the descent I would be ready to go again, having gotten over this little blip.

Back down the road, Richard had died a thousand deaths. He'd shot his bolt, the man with the hammer had got to him, you get the drift. He was steadily getting slower and slower. His new tactic of sprinting two hundred metres in a huge gear and then jumping off for a breather didn't seem like a winner but he soldiered on to the top of the Saises where he was caught by the broom wagon on the descent which ordered him to stop and pull over. They stripped him of his number and time transponder like they do in the real Tour De France and he climbed with feigned regret into the back of the bus. I say feigned because he later told me he was smiling on the inside, knowing that the suffering was over.

I meanwhile had ridden to the base of the col de Aravas. This turned out to be an easier climb. The road really didn't ramp up to any degree and there was a huge flat section in the middle. At one point I was cycling along with a saucy looking French girl wearing very high riding shorts which were creeping a little too far north and needed adjusting. I should have advised her but fatigue made it difficult to talk so I let her carry on in peace whilst I took in the view.

The last few kilometres dragged on but I decided for the first time in the event to put a bit of power down and I started to go past quite a few riders. People were lining the roads outside their chalets holding out cold mineral water for riders to take. I took a bottle from a girl who ran alongside me for a moment. I then threw the water down my back as I had seen Michael Boogered do to a teammate in Le Tour. Owwwww the shock almost gave me a heart attack.

Top of the Aravis. More food. More toilet. The descent from the Aravis seemed to pass quite quickly after the mini break and at last

I seemed to be getting the hang of the Alpine downhills. I was overtaking quite a few riders on the straights but more importantly on cornering as well, and especially on the outside of hairpin bends which required a bit of courage.

Just before the Colombiere loomed into view I stopped to take off my jacket and do the usual bathroom visit. By now I had the bladder of a small mouse with prostate issues.

I stood staring at the beast in front of me and developed a brief plan. My legs still felt pretty good, I hadn't really pushed myself so far due to being a bit apprehensive about my lack of familiarity with the terrain, the distance, the very hot weather and complete lack of cycling talent. I had to make a decision; do I spin and drag myself up within seconds of the time limit or do I go for it? I decided I may as well go for it.

I started the Colombiere in 53x19, a big gear, for show and about twenty seconds later I changed into the small ring. The start of the Colombiere didn't seem too hard and by spinning my gears I started to pass riders. The heat was pretty awful by this stage but I felt strangely good. I looked at a few cyclists' faces and I realised that all of these guys, to a man, were as shot as I was which made me more confident. I came across some American guys dressed in US postal gear riding four abreast. I made a smart alec comment about Armstrong and went past. This went on for the next nine kilometres, going past people like they were standing still and I wished I had been able to do it earlier.

I was flying up the mountain like Pantani in his prime. All I needed was a couple of earrings and a bandana. The climbing was effortless and my legs powerful. The moment was almost spiritual as I felt my breathing and heart rate combine in perfect harmony. Nothing on this last stretch of alp could stop me. Nothing that is, aside from the man with the hammer.

I had become somewhat over-confident in my abilities. Within seconds I wasn't riding like Pantani at all, more like Pavarotti. The road steepened, I was slowing down and my legs were beginning to hurt. I looked to my right and saw the most horrendous sight in front of me, a two kilometre vertical wall. I thought to myself, and apparently so did virtually everyone else:

'It can't be done. How can I have been so near and yet so far? I'm not going to get up that.'

I'd already changed into 39x27, my lowest gear, and now my mouth was wide open gasping for breath. I crawled past people for the next kilometre until I saw a sign saying there was only one more kilometre to go.

Relief, you would have thought but no, the road ramped up even steeper. I tried getting out of the saddle but decided that sitting down like Ullrich and churning the gear, diesel-like, would be a better idea.

Two riders slowly crawled past me. I tried to tag on the back but the proverbial elastic snapped. People at the side of the road were screaming and shouting 'Allez, Allez!' It really wasn't helping.

Through the cacophony of noise I heard a woman's shout.

'One hundred metres to go!' She had a thick French accent.

Yes please. Nearly there.

My eyes were transfixed to the road, knowing I was seconds away from glory. I was going to make it. I rode another minute or so.

'How much bloody longer?'

I then saw a mark on the road which said '200 metres'. Aaaaaaaahhhhhhhh that bastard French woman was lying!

By now I was making weird and wonderful noises from the effort. I don't know how I carried on riding those final few metres without falling sideways. They were far and away the worst two hundred metres of my life on a bike. But I made it to the top the climb. Done.

The relief was huge. There was only a downhill left and even a tourist like me could go downhill. By now I'd had enough and I decided to forget the water and food and just stick the jacket on and fly down the mountain. The Colombiere was by far the most technical descent of the four mountains with plenty of 'fly off the edge' opportunities which, judging by the ambulances I saw happened to more than a few riders. I now started to enjoy the descent, finally allowing the possibility to creep into my mind that I might actually finish the epic journey.

I caught up with another two riders and the three of us went through the valley town together and started a pace line to stop anyone catching up. The red kite came into view. One kilometre to go.

Crowds at the side of the roads roared us on. A couple of left and right turns passed by and a sign showed fifty metres to go. The two guys in front started to blow kisses to the crowd. Sneakily I sprinted past both and gave a Virenque style salute to the crowd with a one fingered kiss and then a fist pump. Oh why not. Hands then came off the handlebars and I raised them both in the air.

I had finished in over seven hours and about halfway down the field. I was hours behind the winner but I had my little moment of glory and it felt very good. Some people were very emotional at the finish and I would love to say that I was too, but instead I was frantically searching for food.

Richard appeared four hours later after having a nice comfortable ride on the bus. Once he arrived back in Britain he threw away the bike, vowing never ever to ride again. I told him it was just an off ride on a long day and he shouldn't give up. Sometimes you're the hammer and sometimes you're the nail. To this day he has not been back on a bike.

For me though this success was the start of something big. I was now a Giant of the Road. The sky was the limit. Who knew what I could achieve next in a stunning career as amateur touring cyclist.

LIKE A VIRGIN CYCLIST
(Chris)

In my first few days in Belgium I was taken to the villages of Kalmthout, Essen, Kapellen, Wildert and Wuustwezel, all in one little corner of north east Flanders, as the show and tell exhibit for Wendy. I was an exotic Australian, the first in the village according to many, and as a result met every available person who had a connection to Wendy: aunts, grandparents, cousins, nieces and nephews, old school friends, university friends, work colleagues and casual acquaintances, all one after the other.

The pattern of every visit was the same. Each rendezvous could be diarized with just two words: 'Meet. Eat'. At every house, apartment, shop, or cafe, for approximately one hour I stuffed my face merrily with mountains of chocolate, koffiekoeken (tasty beautiful custard-filled pastries) and coffee. Belgian frites and beer were often added to the later afternoon and evening visits. All the while I only had to nod and smile when eyes came toward me or when I heard the magic word 'Australia'.

At first I tried to hang on listening to the local babble using the ten words I knew. I had Dutch tapes at home in Australia and I was studying the language but in that first trip I had no chance of joining in. There is a lot of dialect and local language across Flanders, even from village to village, so the few words of Dutch I had learnt were rarely used. Even the word for 'you' which is 'je' in Dutch was never spoken by Wendy or her family or her village. Their version is 'de gij' which is considered the equivalent of 'thou' in English. So really there was nothing to do but eat. Each night we would then roll back to Wendy's parent's house in Essen and let the sugar and fat creep into my storage unit north of pants.

Luckily, on day four Lucien caught me eyeing one of the bikes in the garage. He suggested we go out for a 'real' ride rather than visit yet another third cousin. This is where the fun started.

Being Australian I consider myself close to the perfect athlete. For a small country we seem to excel across the full range of global sports and are by far and away home to the world's best Aussie Rules team. I had seen Lucien in his lycra of course, and knew he rode every other day or so but it meant nothing. Forty years in the saddle? So what. Thirty years of being Australian over here, mate. Bike shmike. How hard could it be?

I put on my trainers and a pair of running shorts and we set off, with my father-in-law leading and me following closely behind. We started out at a nice even pace. After a few kilometers I took a turn in front and began to speed up just a touch. Let us just say I tried to moderately turn the power on, only to demonstrate how young and fit I was. It wasn't about my being boss, just a friendly show of strength. We reached a false flat near a place called Heide and I slipped into a smaller cog. I pushed harder on the pedals and soon felt the strain across my legs and in my lungs. I thought that if I, the Australian, was beginning to tire then poor old Lucien must be about to faint.

Then the problems hit. It didn't take long for me to start puffing, quietly of course, and I eased down a touch. There was no need to hurt him after all. Why prove a point? Wendy would be upset, and what good would it do to embarrass my future father-in-law. My heavy breathing continued and I realized I was also starting to sweat. I could feel my legs struggling to maintain the pace and thought about getting out of the saddle before quickly changing my mind. What if I fell over or some other blunder? It was time to ease off altogether.

I turned around to look at Lucien and was shocked to my laboured core. He was fine. Sparkling. As fresh as the dawn. There was no hint of chest movement or a bead of sweat. Is he taking any air at all? I wondered. He had one hand on the front of the bike and the other was on a mobile phone, sending an SMS or something. Perhaps surfing the web. I didn't think he was contacting emergency services, or at least not for himself anyway. He looked like he could whistle a tune. I quickly gathered gobs-full of air in order to make one clear sentence without it sounding like I was running a marathon. I had to mask the pain.

'So…beautiful…here.'

It was only three words but to make them sound calm and effortless was herculean. More air, must get more air. Calm, be calm. You are fit. More air, but don't inhale deeply, just relax. I had plainly underestimated cycling.

We turned for home shortly afterwards and rode at a relaxing, steady turn. I had time to sit and soak in the scenery and fresh air. It was my first ride on a bike since riding the little BMX of my childhood and I was cooked, but I loved it. We had ridden thirty kilometres, through cornfields and past hedgerows and old churches and village squares and it was incredible. We hardly saw a soul, there was the odd bike and the occasional tractor but that was about it in terms of people.

It turns out the apple doesn't fall far from the tree. My father travelled to Belgium years later and we went out for a ride together. Sure enough two kilometres into the ride I heard from behind in a sixty-five year old voice; 'Here comes Robbie McEwen' and then a flurry of pedal strokes as he went past. We soon slowed right down after that burst of energy.

During what was left of my stay in Belgium on that first trip I went out on the bike every day for the same thirty kilometres round trip. It was hardly Bordeaux to Paris but for me it was an enormous breakthrough. Humble beginnings indeed but the seeds were sown. Aside from being charged by an un-tethered goat riding next to a farm in Essen-Hoek one afternoon it was brilliant.

We travelled home to Australia at the end of the holiday and were soon followed by Wendy's parents. In one sense they travelled all the way to Australia to be there for the birth of our first child. One could also argue that Lucien wanted access to some new roads and rides. True enough to form he bought a bike within two days of arriving in Sydney. Two days. That's not long enough to get over the jet-lag. Those two days of going cold turkey must have hurt the man badly. He bought a mountain bike, a Giant Upland SE. I guess he thought that he was going to be riding on rough country roads wearing an Akubra or cowboy hat.

Lucien took the bike out most days and I envied him on those mornings when our paths crossed. As I was putting on shirt and tie, preparing for the office, Lucien folded maps and drew plans across the breakfast table, looking for new routes, roads and beaches to see and bush trails to tackle.

Most of the rides involved going up and down the northern beaches of Sydney and places in between. The stock standard route usually involved travelling along the beach roads north and then going back home via the national park with a winding six kilometre climb. I had told him he wouldn't see many cyclists out on the roads during the weekdays but I was wrong. He saw lots of riders, all of them friendly he said, with some even commenting on the jersey he wore from his Belgian club as they pulled alongside.

On one of his first rides Lucien had a puncture and stopped to repair it. Two riders also stopped to help him and he was quite perplexed. In Belgium, where men are men quite obviously, you change your own tyre. Nobody stops to assist a simple puncture. He was pleasantly surprised by the experience and told his club-mates back home about the friendly Australian cyclists and their willingness to lend a hand. My future mother-in-law also expressed surprise when she noticed that Australians thank bus drivers with a 'cheers' or a 'ta mate' or a plain 'thank you' when they alight. It's always nice to hear these sorts of comments from visitors to Australia. It's not often that you get a fresh insight on the good manners of your countrymen.

Back in Belgium the following year I took advantage of Lucien's cycling obsession and tackled the age-old challenge of how to ask for permission to marry a daughter the easy way: On a bike. It seemed the thing to do. He didn't eat meals out, thinking it a waste of time, and didn't head to the cafe very often unless it was after a ride so for this type of proposal I wanted to make sure he was at ease and in his element.

We were again cycling through the Heide, near Kalmthout. I had buffered him from a strong north-easterly wind for about twenty kilometres as the gale bent corn fields beside us. I was tired and short of breath and it helped mask the nervousness. I pulled alongside him.

'Ik heb een vraagje. Mag ik met u dochter trouwen?'

I somehow managed to fumble badly what was a well-rehearsed line, and he may have wondered why I wanted to marry his doctor rather than his daughter. In hindsight I should have used her name. Either way he was kind enough to let my gaff slide and gave his blessing in English.

'Yes, if you take good care of my daughter, that's fine.' he said and we turned toward home.

THE CONVERTED
(Chris)

At home in Australia I soon joined the ranks of the cycling obsessed. I bought magazines, books and read blogs and researched the history of recent Tour De France events and I watched highlights of races from the 1990s via the internet. Neil set me straight on Lance and instead encouraged me to look a bit further to guys who lit up the Tour in different ways such as simply having fun by pulling a Big Mac out of a feed bag, or stealing the show through a lone attack up a mountain. Neil sent me some links to old video footage of these 'real giants' featuring guys like Marco Pantani, Miguel Indurain and Michael Boogerd. The Boogey man is the best Dutch rider of the last decade or so and was a particular favourite of Neil's due to his massive crazy Dutch smile and habit of laughing at everything, whether on the road racing or being interviewed or being set up by his teammates. For mid-life cyclists this ability to just enjoy the ride is almost as important as having the latest gear.

Almost. At this point in time I also needed a new bike, and clipless pedals. I was riding the mountain bike Lucien had left behind but it was time to step up to the big league. Unfortunately I also had, and still have a mortgage so my budget could not extend as far as carbon. I scraped together a modest two thousand dollars and bought a Scott Speedster in a size a few centimetres too small, as well as low specification Look pedals and lower specification Shimano shoes.

The purchases were a lower than sea-level start to the gear-buying career of a mid-life cyclist and were treated as such by Neil. When asked by email for an opinion on my selections Neil did not make comment or offer any encouragement whatsoever. I decided the lack of response meant he wasn't aware of the brands but later realized in horror the radio silence was due to something altogether different. Neil was shocked at my cheapness and glad I was riding this 'equipment' ten thousand kilometres away rather than alongside his carbon stallion and five hundred pound sterling shoes.

Clipless pedals were to be the next challenge. No self respecting mid-life cyclist uses flat pedals. The theory is that being connected to the pedals gives a rider increased power and efficiency because as you push down on one pedal you simultaneously pull up with the other. Many physics experts, cyclists and theorists argue that clipless pedals do not offer any real advantage for amateur cyclists and are for show. Show is reason enough for most, including me. Additionally though there is some increased safety benefit with clipless pedals because you are attached to the bike and there is little chance of slipping off the pedal platforms. Of considerably more interest than all of this however is the universally accepted fact that beginners to clipless will have a humiliating, sideways, slow motion fall at some stage. Apparently every newbie has at least one embarrassing and slow collapse to the ground still attached to their bike. This is often at a public place such as a set of traffic lights and is due to the rider forgetting they are locked in. It's a rite of passage.

Luckily for me I was going to be the guy who knew better and through exhaustive research I planned a way to avoid this awkward initiation. On my first ride in clipless I made sure that at every set of lights or intersection I unclipped my left foot about fifty metres before it was necessary. No way was I going down. This defensive style however meant I was always out of the pedal far too early, and as a result I would either coast too often hence dragging down the average speed or I would be forced to turn the pedals when not locked in which saw the stiff sole of the shoe slide all over the place. The pedals took some getting used to but by the end of the first ride, where I managed fifty-two kilometres, I noticed perhaps a modicum of improvement. Unfortunately some fatigue had set in however and the rest can be guessed. Yes, I crashed sideways, very publically, at two kilometres per hour in front of many startled shoppers and a line of traffic. I was five hundred metres from home.

I didn't tell Neil. It is something that doesn't bear thinking about really and is difficult to write down.

The kilometres soon started to flow. Wendy had just given birth to our daughter so we were effectively house-bound and couldn't leave home for more than a few hours, but nap time guaranteed a solid two or three hour window which is the perfect length of time for a night ride around Pittwater and Manly and North Head, or a morning ride up through the northern beaches, or a midday ride through the national park. Surfing sessions down at Manly dropped off conversely, but it was winter anyway and this new found pursuit garnered all of my attention.

I loved riding along McCarrs Creek in particular. The road winds its way up through a national park in Sydney. It is a great ride for a cyclist because the hills work the legs hard while offering short respite here and there as the road ducks through sections of cool shaded rainforest and down short slopes before another climb. The road starts at Bayview, where my parents were living at the time, with its yachts, fishermen, dinghies and pockets of beach and at various points the ride is only a few feet from the water. The route then turns sharply left into the bush, and the first of many small hills forces a change of gear or two before reaching those refreshing dark pockets of palms and gullies. This national park is Australia's second oldest and is only twenty-five minutes from Sydney but is huge and untouched, natural, green and wild and aside from the odd lone cyclist or peloton there is little traffic. Once through the shaded section, the longest part of the climb begins and rainforest gives way to bush, eucalypts and scrub. On a bike you can ride for ten minutes without hearing a noise aside from a waterfall or a cockatoo. Absolute paradise.

Riding in the northern beaches in the spring is not without its dangers however. Cycling alone one day I was in my own world and singing a song in my head, absolutely at peace when I felt a sudden WHOOSH of air and a furious snapping and scratching at my helmet. It was quite a shock, and the associated split-second adrenaline rush caused me to veer sharply and lock the brakes for a second. I knew what it was in an instant. Magpie attack.

To those not used to a magpie assault it is the equivalent of having a chicken, or in this case a turkey, blasted at you from a cannon fitted with a silencer. These strikes have been known to seriously injure cyclists due to sudden swerves into traffic but the giant crow-like enraged birds are generally satisfied with a bloodied ear-lobe or neck. Experts suggest that the attacks have something to do with a combination of nesting, territorial protection, testicles being enlarged and full of testosterone, showing off to partners or just being angry birds in general.

I did what anyone would do in this circumstance which was to tighten my bum, put the hammer down and sprint as fast as possible out of its territory. This particular beast seemingly owned a piece of land the size of a cattle station however and launched two more assaults, an ultra-impressive feat given the super human speed I was laying down. I will point out that this violent assault on my life certainly amused a carload of people who must have wet the car given the amount of laughter coming from inside.

On returning home I investigated potential actions to prevent future injury. One piece of advice was to wear a since discontinued cycling jersey featuring a large image of a winged cyclist on the back. Apparently all types of birds stay away from this one. Continuous head bobbing is another recommendation, as is waving your pump at the beasts for those cyclists who still carry the old style hand pumps. Often though you never see the magpie and instead only hear a swooping noise at the last second before a clash of beak on helmet. So in order to deploy this defence one would have to start head bobbing and arm waving in the middle of the road for no apparent reason which would have created even more entertainment for my new friends in the car. I can't imagine head bobbing fits into Neil's advice of looking the best to be the best so instead I chose the age old method of avoiding the route. Last resort would be riding with an eagle on the handlebars. I will keep this one in reserve.

STRIKER ONE
(Neil)

I'm not entirely sure of the exact moment I got back into cycling and was able to complete the Etape, but I can vividly remember the day I stopped cycling as a youngster. I was aboard a silver beauty known as a Raleigh Striker, bought for me by my parents, and I absolutely loved it.

Unfortunately I was always a little soft-hearted when it came to sharing so when my cousin begged me for a chance to ride it I agreed, thinking little could go wrong. My heart was in my mouth within seconds as I saw him take the name literally and want to strike things, at a worrying pace. He laughed hysterically on leaving a few metres of black tread across the tarmac with a long skid. Uh-oh. My prayers for a safe handover were ignored as he catapulted over the bars on his next trick; the ride into the gutter. My bike, my beloved bike, went crashing to the ground. I ran over to survey the damage while my cousin gingerly got up and dusted himself off.

'Don't worry, Cuz, I'm ok.'

I didn't hear a word he said. I just stared in disbelief at the dent in the stem of my pride and joy. Never again did I allow someone else to ride my bike.

A few months, some car body-filler and a new paint job later, the local kids decided to organise a race up and down a circular stretch of tarmac which climbed up and down the same hill. Five of us lined up, four boys and a girl, giving each other 'The Look' before we took off. Striker only had one gear which inevitably put me at a disadvantage going uphill but I could always stay in contact with the girl. As soon as we turned for the downhill, a series of rapid gear changes from her saw me off the back, dropped like a stone, out into the backdoors of humiliation.

Over time I was able to improve on this and pass the girl and even a few of the boys but I could never finish better than second. I felt like a thin Jan Ullrich.

In the next few weeks I felt an overwhelming need to win at all costs. I attempted in my own unsophisticated way to go faster which generally meant pedalling as if my life depended on it while getting as low on the bike as physically possible.

Of course disaster was just around the corner. It happened on a particularly glorious summer's day whilst streaking down the same stretch of tarmac repeatedly and figuring out how to gain more and more speed.

It almost felt spiritual. I remember thinking to myself I was invincible moments before disaster struck. To this day I'm still not sure what happened next, only that after it ended I was struggling to pick myself up from the ground. Something didn't seem quite right. These were the days before helmets but my head seemed just fine so what was it? I lifted my bike up and realised my arm was backwards.

I tried to lift my bike one handed and wheel it into the house but this proved impossible while supporting a useless arm. The Striker was made from oil rigging pipe after all. I eventually left the bike on the ground and made my way back into the house, only to be confronted by one very angry mother.

'Where is your bike?' She shouted at me as I stood there ashen faced, cradling my mangled arm.

'Er, I left it outside Mum...I think I have hurt my arm.'

'What? You left it outside?' The shouting continued as she stormed off to retrieve the bike, leaving me to wait for her. It was at this point that I looked down and noticed blood dripping from my stomach. How could she not see that?

After a few minutes she returned with my bike and suddenly realised with horror that my arm was positioned at rather the wrong angle. From then my mother went to pieces and alternated between screaming, shouting and crying.

She was trained in first aid but by the time I got to hospital I looked like I had just been exhumed from a tomb in Egypt. I was x-rayed and taken off to theatre where my arm was set, starting what was to become a bit of a saga as it had to be reset months later.

Little did I know at the time but my mum was questioned by staff. You see, for a bike crash, I had unusual injuries. There was no road rash, just a broken arm and a large piece of skin missing on my abdomen. This indicated to the staff some form of physical abuse perpetrated by my apparently volatile mother, whom I should add was normally very kind and gentle but on this occasion was in the throes of shock. I was questioned again about the 'incident' before they released us both.

Inevitably the crash put me off cycling for a while and as much as I hate to admit it, my bottle deserted me when going downhill. I didn't really cycle again until after I left school.

Like most eighteen year olds I was into fads. I used to buy all sorts of equipment and immerse myself into a new sport for a couple of months before jacking it in. Cricket, Chess, Ju-jitsu, Tang soo do, you name it I bought the gear and in most cases had absolutely no idea.

This all changed the day I picked up a mountain bike magazine and saw a basic Trek. The 9000 series I think it was called. That was it, I had to have the bike. In those days it was difficult to find dealers in my local area of Kent which stocked foreign bikes but I eventually found a shop in London.

The sales guy was hopeless and he sold me a bike on the tried and tested sizing formula of 'does it crush your nuts? No? It's perfect then.'

Unfortunately the bike may not have crushed anything but it was way too big and as I subsequently found out, extraordinarily heavy.

This did not stop me from going out and I was soon racking up the miles across the countryside and completing what were enormous rides for me at the time, some thirty kilometres and more. I convinced my mate Dave that he should get himself a new bike as I was growing bored going out on my own, and I wanted to stretch the distances further. I wondered whether the fad could soon be coming to an end.

In Dave's own special way he went out and bought himself a new bike. Of course it wasn't just any bike; it was the model above mine. This was my first introduction to someone buying the best, to look the best, to be the best. That didn't matter too much to my eighteen year old self, years away from middle age, as at least now I had someone to ride with through the fields and woods.

Cycling through the woods was fine but I'm naturally a tidy, organised, picture of sparkling cleanliness and I like my bike to shine. The end of my mountain biking career arrived when I came to a complete stop, brakes caked with mud, and vowed to only ever cycle on the road.

Unfortunately cycling on the road with a mountain bike is hardly a Zen- like experience. The drag of the tyres constantly slows you down and the bike is heavy to move around. I wanted to go faster. The final nail in the mountain bike coffin came when trying to catch up and stay with the local chain gang of road cyclists to annoy them with my mountain version. Ultimately I didn't even get to their back wheel. I was deflated and crestfallen. I was a tourist not a cyclist. Something had to change.

This change occurred in 1998. I had started to watch the Channel 4 highlights of the Tour De France race which began so well for my fellow Englishman, Chris Boardman. Seeing the Super Mario Saeco train blistering along to the end of each stage reeled me further in to road cycling's grip. Obviously I still didn't 'get it' and tried to follow the race and commentary to better understand this 'chess on wheels' as it was being described.

Learn I did however, and eventually the penny dropped that much of cycling is a team sport. I watched in something resembling shock as members of Team Telekom selflessly drove themselves into the ground for Jan Ullrich's chances in yellow when he punctured at the base of a mountain climb.

Michael Boogerd, the charismatic team leader of Rabobank, continued the theme yelling encouragement to Patrick Jonker, his faithful domestique, spurring him on while also pouring water down his back to keep him cool as he lead the peloton up the final mountain of the day.

I continued to remain engrossed in the entire race but there was one stage in particular that sent me to the bike shop. Stage 15 - Grenoble- Les Deux Alpes. Watching a man as fragile in appearance as that bald, bird-like Pantani utterly destroy athletic giants like Ullrich was utterly compelling and made me ask the pertinent questions:

Was I not similarly short?

Was I not also extremely skinny?

Was I not indeed losing my hair?

I had found my calling. I was a born climber. Everyone knew it, but they had striven to keep it from me, fearing that fame would change me and make me forget my humble origins. I had wasted years playing cricket and other pointless sports when all along I had some genius lying dormant and very well disguised within me.

I bought a road bike the day Le Tour finished, and began the incredible journey to cycling novice.

VIVE LE VELO
(Chris)

Aside from the collective efforts of my parents who bought my first bike, Neil who falsified his Etape as a professional athlete discovery event, and my father-in-law with his pair of one million kilometre legs there is one other bike hero requiring some attention. Tim Moore.

Tim did not carry the world before him in a great cycling monument such as Paris Roubaix or win Olympic gold but he achieved something that although humanly possible for a cyclist of modest ability is rarely attempted. He replicated the Tour de France, alone.

By alone I mean completely and wholly un-assisted, without a support car or even a friend beside him apart from the odd fellow cyclist dropping by. Tim attempted every stage of the tour that was scheduled during one particular year. That is, every endless flat, every mountain and every terrifying descent while carrying two spare inner tubes, a credit card and toothbrush. He rode over three thousand kilometres in all sorts of weather, he rode up mountains of fifteen percent gradient and into head winds of up to forty kilometres per hour for twenty one days straight, and completed what can only be described as a monumental achievement.

Those who like cycling and can read will know of his book *French Revolutions* which chronicled those three weeks. Neil recommended the book and I've since read it three times and passed it onto friends. The epic ride appeals on countless levels. Riding through France, tackling mountains, a sense of sporting glory, riding through France a bit more, time off work and eating whatever you like all day and all night. Cyclo-tourists completing just one day's ride often describe knocking off a steak, a pizza and a Mars bar in one sitting and still feeling peckish. Mostly though, I wanted to earn the title afforded to those who complete the tour; Giant of the Road.

In short, it had to be done. I threw the suggestion out to Neil via email and received, not to any great surprise, a rapid and positive response. The emails from London to Hong Kong gathered steam and we agreed to table the proposal to our wives. Wendy said yes immediately. She's Belgian. They ride bikes. Husbands go on holidays to ride bikes. Water is wet. No discussion was needed. His wife however would be slightly more of a challenge than my very own cycle magazine's Miss March. I should add that Wendy mentioned our plan to her father a few days later. He scoffed and guffawed and chortled and clutched his sides and shook with laughter and said disparagingly there is no way we would be able to do it, but more of that later. In the meantime my thoughts were with the Blundells.

The proposal was to pick out a tour route from the next year, 2012, or the year after. We would complete each stage of the pro tour in order, but a few weeks after the pros had been through. The first challenge to be overcome was timing. Neil's wife was up the duff for a change, sorry, happily pregnant for a second time, and doing the maths meant the baby was due a few months before next year's event. We decided on the year after, which was 2013.

Laura, probably sensing it was another hare-brained scheme of Neil's likely to be forgotten, consented.

I should clarify there was never any doubt that we would be able to complete the physical side of things. After all, Tim Moore could do it, and he allegedly started out as an out of shape middle-aged fellow who hadn't ridden a bike for years. We were a skinny Etape-completing untapped genius and a reasonably shaped but still soft in the middle thirty-eight year old. Aside from this we were a team. With Neil up front and me tucked behind out of the elements for twenty-one stages we would have the tour done and in the bag and the Neil and Chris Tour DVD released a few weeks later. It was only three thousand kilometres after all. Forget twenty-one days of potentially blazing sun or torrential rain, mountain passes, massive gradients and head winds of fifty kilometres per hour. We were giants of the road already.

The only problem at this stage aside from cost, time, effort, planning, wives, equipment, legs, family, work, and asking our employers for approval for a month or more off was miles under the belt. We had approximately none. I stretch the truth a little as I was in fact putting away a heroic thirty to seventy kilometres per week on my mountain bike, riding up and down the hills behind our house and not much further.

Neil was also slowly drip-feeding the miles into his legs via a daily commute to and from the station every day. When travelling to work, Neil dresses like Captain Commuter in fluorescent jacket, orange bandana and suit trousers with clips. He rides a typical commuter's regular twelve kilometres or less per day, but he does so in the style of a kamikaze desperate to prove his virility to any other rider daring to share the road. Neil relishes in overtaking road bikes, especially while commuting, even if it means destroying himself in the red zone, taking an unplanned exit after having done so and, in all truthfulness on one occasion, losing his breakfast on the roadside from the exertion. Those he passes become 'commuter kills' or notches on his bike seat post, and each are explained in great detail via daily emails down to the age of the rider, the jersey, the make of bike, speed, and the nod, smile or wave he gave each rider as he casually slid past. Neil also takes care to note and recall any reaction from the rider, such as changing gear or chasing him down. I should say *attempting* to chase him down. The former has never been done according to Neil. This hunting of road bikes is a practise Neil continues to this day when commuting, so riders around the area of Dartford station should consider themselves forewarned.

These twelve kilometre road kills and three kilometre hill climbs, no matter how tiring they were, or tire*some* for those passed by Neil, did not hold us in good stead for two hundred kilometres per day over twenty-one days. The fatiguing and wearing effect of perching on a rock hard three inch saddle day after day is staggering on a professional athlete, let alone two guys who could have been professional athletes but chose to be office workers.

For me the pain usually started at the lower back, after fifty kilometres or so. At the onset of this I would try to relieve what is a dull ache by shifting my body all over the bike and attempt to stretch the back out. Following this, at about the seventy kilometre mark, the neck and shoulders start to register messages of a sharper pain. The hands don't want to be left out either and I flip and flop from the right to the left hand, and then to holding the bike in the middle of the stem or on the drop handlebars or using the tips of my fingers. This is when I reach the unfortunate part of the ride where every move to temporarily relieve one point of pain, usually the point connected to the bike, seems to exacerbate another.

Luckily my rides very rarely exceeded seventy kilometres and on those occasions where I over exerted myself I was able to end the pain by climbing off and lying down. But pain, according to every cycling biography ever written, is a cyclist's friend. Pain is where the true bike giant stands out from the also-rode. Jens Voight, the German pro cyclist of twenty years standing, apparently has a three word mantra when racing that he repeats to himself and growls aloud in an Arnold Schwarzenegger accent while staring at his thighs; 'Shut up legs'. In my case I would need to yell 'shut up legs, and lower back, and the arms you can shut up, and wrists up yours too.'

Basically I would have to get over it, and harden up.

One idea I had in order to combat pain setting in from these all too brief and intermittent rides was to tackle the challenge head-on and do what many cyclists do. Turn to drugs. I could swallow the best to be the best. With no easy access to performance enhancers, I had to research readily available medicines like painkillers and anti-inflammatories. Most schools of thought were that you needed to take copius amounts, they rarely worked or improved the ride and they could ruin your digestive system.

What was evidently required then was time in the saddle. Those same cycling biographies that pontificate about pain as your pal also seem to regurgitate one another's views on there being no substitute for training, and practise making perfect. Still I was non-plussed in spite of the overwhelming written evidence and common sense. The thought of fitting in tonnes of training on weekends and around work hours for a year didn't appeal as much as riding in France for three weeks.

Wendy's father weighed in again from afar and mockingly said that we wouldn't last more than two stages. He thought that in order to ride for three weeks straight one needed to be able to ride for more than three hours straight, and I was yet untested in this regard.

With a young family I loved being around, there was limited time to be spent in lycra on weekends. Let's be clear. I much preferred to be out on the road on my bike in the heat of the day instead of lazing around all summer with a beer and a barbeque and a beach ball or out surfing. This is obvious. But the time just wasn't there. My daughter wanted me around the house. She was young and enjoyed the company of her dad. In time, I was told, she would grow out of this lovely habit and become a teenager and not notice me even while I was standing in front of her with my lips moving and orders coming from my mouth, but for now it mattered that I was home, playing.

I started searching the internet for cycling articles on converting from novice to genius in twenty minutes a week. This theory of limited training also had to be run by Neil who I believed would support my view of giving a little in order to get a lot. We were going to turn the theory of time versus reward on its head. If anyone could be a true cycling god by riding once a month for ten minutes, it was Neil.

Neil agreed. I knew he would. The path to greatness could be as short as a morning commute, he said.

FRAGRANT HARBOUR
(Chris)

Shortly after the training plan was agreed my family and I were relocated abroad. There were to be no more rides along Barrenjoey Road in Sydney, counting off the northern beaches one by one and deciding whether to have a quick dip then or later. We were going to Asia, so instead of beach I was going to get jungle. Concrete jungle, specifically, as we were moving to Hong Kong.

We stayed for the first few weeks in a serviced apartment close to a part of Hong Kong called the Gold Coast. In terms of the name, I can say there was definitely a coast. It was the last stop on the train line heading west on the Kowloon side of Hong Kong and aside from aesthetic shortcomings, the Gold Coast was also a bit too far from work. For our more permanent home we eventually settled on a place called Sai Kung.

Sai Kung is a small village on the Kowloon side of Hong Kong. According to locals, Sai Kung cannot really be translated into any meaningful words. Sai means 'west' and Kung is a type of Taiwanese fish ball, so the literal translation could be 'Taiwanese fish ball in the west'. This might describe the smell from the old part of town in a summer's evening but doesn't seem right somehow. Anyway, what is certain is that Sai Kung is a former fishing village, and is referred to as the garden of Hong Kong. We chose this place because it sounded green and appealing and we were a little apprehensive about living thirty storeys up in a tenement block close to the city. We wanted to avoid the idea of our three year old pressing her face up against the window looking at concrete towers opposite, wanting to go outside. It also meant I could go cycling.

I should add we also chose Sai Kung because of the rolling, screaming, thunderous, kicking tantrums our daughter threw on the three occasions we had planned to look at other parts of Hong Kong. At one point she was lying on the floor of City Super, a stylish supermarket in Causeway Bay, screaming, break-dancing and moving her body in a circle like the hand of a clock. Of all the places we had planned to visit; Discovery Bay, Clearwater Bay, Happy Valley, Tin Hau, Sai Kung and Deepwater Bay we only managed to get a reasonable tantrum-less look at Sai Kung. So Sai Kung it was.

I went out on my first ride the day after we arrived in Sai Kung. Purists will be upset at the one day delay and it can't be adequately explained but I am sure it had something to do with tiredness from the move, or laziness. As I pulled away from the house I was buzzing. These streets, after all, were going to be where I started out as a middle aged man in lycra and blossomed into a middle aged Giant of the Road in lycra. I didn't know what to expect on the ride aside from crazy drivers, one hundred percent humidity, typhoons, hills and lung busting heat. Oh, and snakes.

There is De Rosa and there are snakes in Hong Kong of the slithering kind. Lots and lots of them. This is a country that has managed to house seven million people in about ten football fields so cramming in ten times as many snakes is no problem. We were told that snakes were common, especially around Sai Kung where we lived, and most were harmless. There was the odd cobra that apparently came closer to urban areas and was nothing to be alarmed about. Everyone seemed to have a cobra story, with the occasional 'king' word thrown in for good measure. King cobras are the longest venomous snakes in the world, growing to five metres. I spent a few hours researching snakes and Hong Kong, while at home in Sydney, and managed to find that yes, there were a lot of snakes, and yes, there were a lot of venomous snakes, but thankfully attacks on humans were uncommon.

In thirty or so years in Australia, a country known for the odd deadly animal or two, I only managed to enjoy close encounters in the wild with three snakes. One was a red-bellied black snake on a footpath in Noosa. The second was a small grey snake on a bush track in the Blue Mountains and the third was an eastern brown snake lying right at the side of a quiet road at the top of North Head in Manly as I sped past on my bike. This last encounter gave me something to think about for the next few kilometres as I wondered whether snakes could leap at cyclists or if their fangs would pierce cycling shoes, or whether on busy roads I should prepare for sudden snake strikes and accept these rather than swerve into traffic.

In Hong Kong I managed to double this personal snake tally in the first few weeks. About three kilometres after setting out I came across a very large and very stretched out snake. It was lying across the road looking perfectly green with the exception of its head which had the colour and texture of minced beef (though I am sure it tasted like chicken). A CSI investigation was unnecessary in determining the cause of death because the distinct corrugated tyre mark above the neck line told the story. The snake was halfway up a slight climb and I was travelling slowly enough to have a good old rubberneck at the poor thing.

I continued on for another kilometre or so, again mulling over snake vs. bike battle theories as well as the snake's genus and whether it was venomous. I tried to recall the internet searches while keeping my mind off cadence, heat, neck pain and how many kilometres were left. A second snake then appeared along the side of the road. This one was smaller and grey, and not at all like the first except that it was also very dead. At this point in time I wondered whether there was a plague.

I reached the summit and started the descent. Lo and behold a little olive green snake rapidly wriggled across the road. This time I had to brake sharply to avoid sending him off to see his friends in the great terrarium in the sky. It disappeared into thick scrub at the side of the road.

This third snake shook me up a little more than the first two, partly due to its still having a head and the ability to move at pace, but mostly due to its being the third snake in ten minutes. I had my eyes widely peeled for the rest of the journey, barely watching the road while scanning the jungle verge for leaping king cobras and other exotic cyclist killers lurking in the Hong Kong shadows.

The second ride trumped the first.

I was riding up Chuk Yeung Road in Sai Kung. Scottish pro rider David Millar spent his teens in this part of Hong Kong and lived only a few kilometres away. In his biography, David mentions by name a lot of the roads around Sai Kung and the fun he had hanging on to buses and the fun he also had trying to sprint up these hills to the point of illness but Chuk Yeung Road does not get a mention. I would like to think it is because he avoided the challenge.

Chuk Yeung road is just over two kilometres in length, all of it uphill, and most of it around twenty percent gradient. Instead of writing a boring description of its steepness I will just say that it is a bastard of a hill. Especially when it is thirty-eight degrees Celsius, sunny, ninety-eight percent humid, you are on a Giant Upland SE mountain bike potentially weighing more than you do, and it is the second time you have ridden the hill that day. Additionally, for some reason, there were trail walkers out in the heat. Ordinarily on a bike you should be able to pass a walker at pace and disappear into the distance. On Chuk Yeung Road however this took some doing, especially if you wanted to make it look effortless and thoroughly relaxing as you casually float by even though you are on the rivet and just about to pop.

I had just passed two sweaty trail walkers, who were complete with umbrellas, visors, walking sticks, camel backs, the whole kit and caboodle, and I crested the peak of the climb. I rolled to the side of the road, completely out of breath. I was panting and red-faced, no, purple-faced, and my temple was throbbing. I fumbled with the hot water bottle stuck in the cage and there he was, eyeballing me. It was the biggest and baddest bike eating snake of the lot. King cobra. He was coiled tightly by the side of the road and looked like two stacked grey car tyres with a head on top. A sort of Michelin snake.

I said two words; the last was 'me' and stepped back to the other side of my bike in about one-tenth of a second. My flight or fight response had worked and flight was the clear winner.

Luckily this king cobra also seemed disturbed enough by the sight of my panting purple lycra person and he too made a retreat, though somewhat more laissez-faire than mine, to the safety of the bush. At this point the two trail walkers appeared and wondered why I was a mix of purple and white and staring into the jungle. That is until they saw the great grey crocodile sliding off. One of them started swiftly snapping away with a camera from a safe distance.

I walked off and began the descent back down, again with eyes like saucers.

Mel, our neighbour's maid, had a similar encounter. She was outside washing the car one afternoon in late summer when she went within a flicker of a cobra's tongue. She reached down behind the car to put a sponge in a bucket of water when the snake reared up at her and hissed. Mel jumped back about two feet with a yelp, holding her hands to her chest.

Luckily for Mel a pair of local removal men were working at the house next door and just happened to be standing next to their truck, parked a few feet away from the cobra. On hearing the squeal they both casually walked over to the car and saw the snake which was now defensively curled up against a retaining wall. The elder of the two picked up a broom that was lying nearby and swung it down hard twice on the cobra's head. He then ground away at the head of the limp snake with the heel of his sturdy removalist's boot before picking it up and slinging it onto his truck. He told the maid he was going to make soup.

Although I was at work that day I asked Mel to repeat the story to me about five times just to hear how high the thing rose up off the ground. The answer varies between about one and two feet. Though she never mentioned a change of underwear I wouldn't have been surprised.

There was one other significant brush with nature on the bike worth documenting, and this occurred only a few days after the King.

It was a summer's day in Hong Kong. No more needs to be said about the ball-tearing heat. I had ridden forty kilometres on the mountain bike and was heading into the Sai Kung Country Park which is a sort of national park complete with trails, picnickers, camping sites and waterfalls. Sweat was pouring off in the usual constant drip from the centre of my helmet. The arms were wet and the hands sticky. My back was saturated and my face was once again hovering in the red zone, ready to upgrade to purple. I reached the bottom of one of the small hills before entering the park and I dropped down a gear. A swarm of local Cantonese cyclists appeared on the other side of the road, coming in the opposite direction.

I did my usual wave from the right-side handle bar to these fellow cyclists and nodded as they flew past in a hurry. The leader called out to me;

'How's the head?'

I was puzzled. What did he say?

I repeated it to myself.

'How's the head?'

What did he mean by that?

Was my helmet off to one side? I reached up and moved it around. No, it felt fine, couldn't be the helmet.

Why was he asking about my head? Was he having a go at my purple face? How could he tell at that speed, from where he was, on the other side of the road, that I had a very purply red face? Maybe if he rode alongside me like Andy Schleck up the Galibier, looking directly into my eyes could he see how close I was to breaking? This couldn't be right. Not from there. Anyway, I thought, stuff that. I actually *am* on the rivet. I am pushing a big gear up a hill, and am riding close to my limit. I'm not ashamed to admit it, and it is Hong Kong after all. In the summer too, thank you very much. I am entitled to look a bit red-faced. It shows just how hard I was working, unlike him quite clearly.

So I had worked it out. 'How's the head?' must have been referring to my purple-ness.

Still, it just didn't feel right. I kept on riding and analysing. Well, he was either talking about my gasping look, or was letting me know that I would have some sort of a headache today given how hot it is in Hong Kong when out on a bike. Or a bit of both maybe. I took a swig from my water bottle.

Even so, it was a bit of a strange thing to yell out across the road on a bike. How's the head?

I think I pushed myself harder for a few minutes after this little episode, working my way up the climb. I was frustrated at not being able to understand the point of the comment no matter how benign it was. I crested the hill and sped into the descent.

It didn't take long however before I was abruptly snapped out of further scrutiny by yet another creature of the jungle. Halfway down the slope and turning through a sharp left hand bend covered in shadows I was suddenly forced to grab hard at the brakes. The back wheel slid out slightly with a short screech.

There was a herd of wild buffalo on the road. I should be honest here; they were actually big black wild cows with pointed horns rather than ordinary run-of-the-Serengeti-mill buffalos. They were all standing in the middle of the road, ogling me. Some pre-historic natural instinct made me instantly lock eyes with the biggest. He was staring right back at me and chewing whatever he had in his mouth, maybe a pair of Oakley Radar Path Livestrong sunglasses. Luckily in spite of the locked brakes I still had enough momentum to swerve, duck and steer through the herd without incident and I made a swift exit to safety.

It took around fifty metres for the penny to drop. The cyclist from a few minutes ago had actually yelled out 'Cows ahead', not 'How's the head?'

I got the award for biggest clown that day.

Things grew worse on the return home as I had the added distraction of a clicking noise when applying the back brake. Once in the garage I had a quick look at the caliper and being an Australian male knew instantly what to do. Take it to the shop.

In Australia if I wanted a mechanical problem fixed on my bike the experience was deflating. The owner of the local bike shop was Bike Nazi. He was tough, he was short, and he had calves bigger than my thighs. He was British and had the aura of an ex-track star on the run from gambling debts in South London. One withering look at my crappy little cheap bike and moderately hairy and skinny legs was enough for us to agree our relationship. Sure, I could have gone further afield to bike shops new but there weren't many within an acceptable distance from home, and these were often also supported by similar intimidating angry bike people with little time for duffers on cheap alloy bikes.

Inevitably I had to steel myself even just to make a phone call and beg for an appointment. I was sure he would be able to tell from my voice I was a hairy legged cycling pretender Fred. I had to be apologetic, accept condescension with good grace, of course find a time that worked in with him and listen with sorrow or tut-tut as he told me how busy he would be for the coming weeks. Sure, I can wait. Of course, I understand. You have a business to run. Following this I had to prepare for the inevitable sucking of teeth as the payment of filthy lucre was discussed.

Moving to Hong Kong gave me a chance to re-invent the whole bike shop experience and I was pretty happy with the results. The bike shop in Sai Kung was the polar opposite to that of its counterpart in the northern beaches of Sydney. The first difference, albeit a chasm, was the size. It was a tiny little one hundred square feet of a shop.

When it came to service, timeliness, availability, and dare I say it, friendliness, the little shop of bikes in Sai Kung was however a giant of the road. I could take my bike down there whenever I wanted. Sunday at 11am? No worries. Tuesday at 10pm? Sure. Saturday night? Whatever, it didn't matter.

The young local mechanic/owner/salesman/expert/handyman would always be perched on a red wooden stool at the front of the shop with a cigarette hanging out of his mouth. He was often playing with a yappy little dog tied to a pole or talking to an old lady on a second red stool at the other side of the shop. Bike kit lay everywhere. Bike frames hung from the ceiling and complete bikes were lined up at the back door. There were pumps, tyres, tubes, tools, stands, helmets, levers, chains and rings in every inch of space.

'Hi mate, I need new brakes please.'

'Sure no problem, la.'

'La' in Hong Kong is the equivalent of 'mate'. The cigarette bobbed around his mouth.

'How much is that?'

'Fifty dollars, la.'

This was around six US dollars.

'Great, when can I pick it up?'

'Ahhh no need, la. Wait here. Do now. Mmmm. Okay, la.'
Within seconds he stripped the old brakes off, lined the new
ones, ran a quick test, re-aligned them, tested them again, tweak,
done. The cigarette was still alight.

In our first year in Sai Kung I went to the shop at least a dozen
times, often just for the hell of it when I didn't really need
anything. I changed the tyres on three bikes, bought helmets,
bought kid's bikes, got the gearing fixed, replaced the chain and
had some new cranks installed. After each visit I would go home
and brag to Wendy about the ease of the whole thing as well as the
service, how clever the guy was, the unbelievably low price, and I
wondered how the shop could make any money. I would have paid
them triple and still been miles ahead.

One gloomy Sunday afternoon however the party ended. At first
glance it looked like all was well. Bike guy was sitting there on his
little red wooden stool, he had a cigarette stuck to his lips and the
old lady was hovering in the corner. But there were no bikes. It
was a shell of a shop. The shutters were up and the shop was open
but inside there was nothing apart from concrete walls and a slab.
He saw me coming towards him, wheeling my daughter's bike, and
he watched me as I stopped in slow motion from about ten metres.
He waved me away and shook his head a couple of times. The old

lady stared at me, as did a couple of other locals that were standing around and I left, as gutted as the bike shop.

There was only one other bike shop in Sai Kung. On entry for the first time, bike in hand, I was a little wary, and I wondered whether the first shop was only a rarity. The Cantonese word for a Caucasian is gweilo which loosely translates as 'white ghost'. In Hong Kong as a gweilo you can find yourself being wholly ignored and transparent to the locals, or the reverse and being treated royally. This royal treatment can extend to being handed a regal bill. Perhaps the assumption is that westerners can afford to pay more. To my great relief however the second bike shop in Sai Kung seemed to follow the practice of the first and the service was fast, cheap and effective. At that point I knew I needed to concentrate on learning a few simple mechanical fixes. Eventually we would move back to Sydney and aside from the expense I wanted to avoid a re-acquaintance with an older and meaner Bike Nazi down the track.

HARD SHOULDER
(Chris)

In March, Wendy and I planned a return holiday to her parent's home in Essen for the European summer. During one of their frequent phone conversations, Lucien told my wife that I should come along for a ride with his club on the weekend of my arrival. There was a catch though. He said I had to do some training first.

To Wendy, this invitation was a massive deal and one I could not turn down. She told me not to embarrass myself. As I edged closer to this big Flemish test I knew I had to get more miles under the belt and in particular do some longer one-day rides. The longest I had ever ridden was about seventy kilometres which is not great preparation for a ride against seasoned, wily and performance-enhanced elderly Belgians.

I set about attempting my first eighty kilometre ride, with the view to gradually building up to rides of one hundred and twenty kilometres or so. One small hurdle was getting onto and safely using the treacherous roads around my house for that sort of distance. Hong Kong has no time for road bikes. They do not belong. For the locals a bike should either be a full suspension mountain bike ridden on a purpose built, child friendly cycling path with a family of five in tow, or be made just after the invention of the penny farthing and used for carting chickens. Road bikes belong on a track at the Olympics.

Space and time are also in short supply in Hong Kong. Generally speaking, you need to take things from your fellow countrymen rather than expect them to share. Whether you are in a queue at the bank, looking for a spare table in a restaurant or reaching for the last orange at the fruit market you need to stake out your territory, push and shove, and bring out your inner beast. If not you will be walked all over, even by the littlest of little old ladies. The same applies on the roads. If you are a driver you will soon learn that you will be spared no quarter or afforded the slightest gesture to creep into a gap or turn onto a road. You need to force your way in. Bash and barge. This is all well and good when you are in a Jeep Cherokee with a bull bar but on an eight kilogram bicycle in lycra your options are limited.

Added to this of course is the lack of hard shoulders on the roads in Hong Kong, particularly around where we lived. Every square inch of land in the country is divided up and squared away with nothing wasted. The roads were fashioned for cars, trucks, buses and the occasional cow. Bikes were not mentioned when plans were drawn up and the land designated for use. So the road is made of two lanes going in each direction, together with a very hard looking concrete retaining wall on either side. There is little margin for error and I was about to find this out the hard way.

The route I had chosen for my first long ride was from Chuk Yeung Road where we lived to an area deep in the Sai Kung country park. I thought this wouldn't be too bad in terms of driver avoidance. Not completely safe, but not running with the bulls. I would dodge most of the traffic as I would be heading away from the city and, after all, it was a country park. Surely drivers on the way to the 'garden of Hong Kong' were bound to be peaceful nature lovers on a jaunty weekend picnic.

In terms of distance the route was to cover ten kilometres into the park and up to a reservoir. From there I would turn around, ride back to the original departure point, and repeat. It was a bumpy route with a few small hills along the way and a sharp two kilometre climb at the end. In total the ride was to be four laps of the twenty kilometre circuit. I wanted to average twenty-eight kilometres per hour which would be a massive haul considering fitness levels were as lumpy as the ride.

After the first two laps I was down on the planned average speed but feeling well and confident and not on the receiving end of the usual lower back pains. The new tweak to my riding style was staying in the saddle at all costs and it was paying dividends.

During these initial forty kilometres I only had one run in. That was with a street sweeper who let his large broom drop horizontally from the footpath to a level of oh, let's just say about the head of your average cyclist. The universally understood primal scream 'Oi' encouraged him to pull the broom back onto the path. Incidentally he yelled 'Oi' straight back at me, perhaps upset at my rude outburst.

In terms of cars, there had been no physical altercation, yet, and I had even learned a new habit from the local drivers. They like to honk their horn to let you know when they are directly behind you. They also like to honk their horn to let you know they are about to pass, and they like to honk their horn as they come right alongside you. I'm sure they do this by way of courtesy so I won't complain but the first honk or two had me a tad jumpy in the saddle. Following this the nerves settled and with every massively disturbing horn honk I managed a little wave from the handle bar by way of thanks while quietly mumbling words to the contrary.

I had of course made sure I was highly visible, and wore an outrageously colourful cycling shirt to announce my presence on the road. While this did the trick, it didn't take long to work out that aside from the horn blasts I would also have to deal with the extremely limited patience of drivers. Most seemed content to pull in behind and mull over a course of action rather than immediately hurtle around at speed. This is when the trouble starts as the cars would creep out from behind, very close to my rear wheel, and if they see something coming the other way they dart back in. The longer they sit behind the shorter their patience gets, and the more risks they take. Thirty seconds is the average limit. After half a minute that's it, they've had enough; they just pull out no matter where you are and no matter what is coming the other way. They take over the lane.

On completion of the third lap, at the sixty kilometres mark, my confidence levels were still high. Although the average speed was down I still felt great in the saddle and was turning reasonable gears on the hills, I even managed to pass a road bike close to the summit of the last climb.

This confidence was about to plunge. I was going slightly downhill on a dip in the road just before a roundabout. I was travelling at thirty-five kilometres per hour. For some reason I pulled a little on the brakes. I think I could feel that a car behind me was about to perform the "I've-had-enough-I've-got-a-picnic-to-get-to" manoeuvre. At the point where he overtook me unfortunately a car also happened to be coming in the opposite direction. This forced him to veer back onto me and boom, I went down.

My mother would be pleased to know that instead of swearing as I flew over the handlebars like a sack of potatoes I instead managed a solemn and polite growl.

'Oh no.'

I lay across the road on my back. The car that hit me stopped.

From where I was lying I could see there was a bus behind me, about two metres from my feet. The engine was idling.

Tuk tuk tuk tuk tuk tuk tuk tuk.

The driver was sitting there staring at me with his hands on the steering wheel. I noticed he had turned the bus hazard lights on, probably to warn other motorists there was a dead westerner needing to be swept away.

Part of me wanted to get up but the rest of me was saying that it was quite comfortable just lying on the road and there was no rush. I lifted my head slightly off the ground. The car that had hit me then drove off. He or she must have been waiting for signs of life and my head movement was confirmation.

I slowly lifted my shoulders from the road and looked at the hole in my elbow. Ow. My back hurt and the shoulder too. My knee was bleeding. Need to move. I leaned forward, then stood up and shuffled to the footpath, dragging my bent bike behind me. I started to do the inventory. There was a lot of blood from the shoulder, the elbow, the knee and the shin, but nothing seemed broken. Phew. Through some good deal of fortune during the accident I had attempted to shoulder charge the road on my right hand side rather than reach out with my hands. My collar bone, the most commonly broken bone amongst cyclists, was intact.

Two Filipinas ran over to where I was standing.

'Are you ok?'

'Yes, I think so.'

I took a sip from my water bottle. I noticed my hand was shaking.

'I think you need an ambulance. You should sit down.'

'Thanks. I'm OK. I just need to stand for a minute.'

The traffic started up in earnest now and there was a good deal of rubbernecking at me and my blood.

'I got the number plate. He just drove into you. We saw it.'

'Oh great, thanks. He, umm, he's gone. He stopped. I saw he stopped. Better write the number plate down somewhere please, if you wouldn't mind.'

'It was NM 42..' She was abruptly cut off by her friend.

'No, it was MN 2442.'

Oh dear.

"No. I'm sure it was NM 44 something."

We got no further with the number plate. I reported it to the police later that day but I was only able to remember the type of car and the colour. Without the number plate the car would be impossible to trace.

A few hours later I was stitched up and bandaged in the hospital. The elbow wound, complete with bone chip, became infected as predicted by hospital staff and took on a nice balloon shape requiring antibiotics over the coming days. Less frightening than the crash but worth noting is the enormous volume of pills which were handed to me from the hospital dispensary. They gave me antibiotics, sleeping pills, painkillers, anti-inflammatory pills, anti-histamine tablets, aspirin, vitamins, and the piece de resistance; pills to combat the indigestion I would get from taking so many pills.

In all there was no major physical damage but my self-assurance on Hong Kong roads had diminished even further. My first long Hong Kong ride in preparation for tackling the Belgians, an event which was only two months away, had gone very badly.

I needed some counsel from Neil as to the new plan of attack. This was a man who had a few crashes under his belt after all. He would know what to do. I told him I was going to stick to training indoors.

'There's a saying isn't there, Macman? You have to get back on your bike. You might have heard it before, even in Australia.' Neil attempted sympathy.

'I guess so. I am not really worried about getting on the bike to be honest. I've never had a stack in Belgium or in Australia. I don't think I will have a problem there. I just, you know, don't feel that great about taking on the local drivers again.'

'OK aside from being a smart arse I should say I actually read somewhere that you really do need to get back on the bike or else your confidence will be shot. We are going to be riding the Tour de France in less than a year, how do you think I can get through the mountains if you are not in front buffeting me from the wind the whole way.'

'Like I say, I have no problems about getting back on, just not here. These people are psychopaths.'

'But you're not going to Europe for months. Unless you are ready to taper off the training you should probably go for a short ride, just until you feel you can get out on your bike without getting smashed.'

He was right. I couldn't taper when I hadn't even really gotten started. I had to get back on.

The new plan was ride to the mountain bike only. The road bike and bent wheel were mothballed. I would complete at a minimum one long ride a week, and preferably two, which had to be for at least three hours come rain, hail or shine. The foot paths where we lived were very wide and hardly used by pedestrians so I could get on these and then hop off when people were around. In this way I could avoid most of the traffic. I had seen one person get fined by local police for riding on the footpath and I could take the risk. The fine would be a few dollars at most.

The plans for tackling the Tour de France together were in place, and I was going to prepare for the challenge by riding the footpaths of Hong Kong on a mountain bike.

NO MORE MR. NICE GUYS
(Chris)

Neil soon insisted that we get some significant cycling hours under the belt. With just over twelve months to go until the big event we had to get serious. We set ourselves an initial target of five hundred miles per month.

These five hundred miles, or around eight hundred kilometres in metric terms, could take the form of either an ordinary road ride or sitting on a trainer. Computers don't work on cheap trainers like mine because the front wheel is stationary so our schedule assumed that one hour on the trainer equated to twenty five kilometres on the road. The effort put in on a trainer is often considered to be twenty percent harder than a road bike as you constantly need to grind away at the pedals without a break or free-wheeling opportunity usually afforded on the road. The twenty-five kilometre number was therefore conservative, but it was also fair as we were protected from hills, wind, rain and attacks from De Rosa.

So we had a plan. We would complete eight-hundred kilometres a month for six months and then ratchet the numbers up gradually at a total yet to be agreed for the following eight months. A cautious estimate would see us bag around fifteen-thousand kilometres of riding before tackling the tour.

Better news was that I had recently moved the family to Discovery Bay on Lantau Island. The roads in Discovery Bay are free of cars. People move around on golf carts or buses. These golf carts can cost up to one hundred and fifty thousand US dollars for a licence so there are not many of those. Additionally there is good access to flatter roads around the airport which are also relatively free of traffic. It is the best area in Hong Kong for cycling.

The first week was ridiculous. It was too easy. I started the week with a pre-dawn Saturday ride of sixty kilometres comprised of three hilly, car-free laps of the roads around Discovery Bay. I was out of the house for a little over two hours and back in time to have breakfast with my daughter. The Sunday plans also ran smoothly. I spent the morning with my daughter taking her for a ride on a scooter from one end of Discovery Bay to the next including a nice, long and reasonably steep hill.

We had lunch together with my wife and then it was time to get back out on the saddle again though this time it was with my daughter who wanted a crack at the hill on her own bike with me alongside. Unfortunately these miles didn't count for my legs as I was barely pedalling but I must say the proud father in me enjoyed watching her refuse to give up, even when threatened with the dreaded backwards roll as the hill rose steeply in front of her.

The usual Hong Kong rains and storm arrived in the late afternoon. A combination of the weather and hours of exercise for my daughter meant it was time for a bit of Tom and Jerry. In my case that meant Cadel and Andy. The television in the spare room was turned on to a Tour de France DVD and the trainer mounted. I cranked out two hours which meant another fifty kilometres in the bag.

This fifteen-thousand kilometre plan was turning into a lark. Luckily for me I quite enjoy the trainer. In Australia I struggled with being indoors and always wanted to be out on the road but in Hong Kong, with the limited choice of roads, and the drivers, and the heat or rain I needed alternatives and grew to love it. Cycling DVDs made an enormous difference too as did the industrial-strength air conditioning unit pointed at my face like a million pound wind tunnel.

I had completed one-hundred-and-ten kilometres in two days with only the merest of impositions on family time. I raced through a few more sessions on the trainer after work that week and reached the one-hundred-and-eighty kilometre target with a day to spare. I could see I was turning from a mid-life cyclist into a potential pro. Confidence was high. If the Australian Institute of Sport had a Hong Kong branch I would have popped in for a VO2 test.

The second week was a carbon copy of the first, even down to the scooter and bike ride with my daughter in the morning and the Tom and Jerry, Cadel and Andy show in the afternoon. With a Tuesday and Thursday session on the trainer I had another successful week tucked away. I also added an extra half hour on to the last session, meaning I was ahead. Unbelievable. A crowd would have been roaring.

The next week I proudly talked through the plan with a non-cycling but very mid-life South African friend. He furrowed his brow a little.

'What's a trainer? An indoor thing?'

'Yes. It sits under your bike connected to the back wheel and holds the front wheel off the ground. So you are on a road bike rather than exercise bike.'

'Is that as hard as riding?'

'Yes and no. Well, more yes than no. I am in the big ring up front and practically the smallest cog in the back so, you know, I am really pushing it. And it only counts as twenty-five kilometres per hour when it is actually probably a lot more than that.' The excuses seemed ready-made somehow.

'It's not though, is it? Not as hard, I mean.'

I stared at him.

He added, 'Don't you think you should be practising on the road, especially if you plan on riding for three-thousand kilometres or whatever it is. If it were me, I would be on the road. There's no substitute, mate. My grandmother could do an hour on an exercise bike and she's no longer with us. Wouldn't it be better to be in the elements, rain hail or shine? I thought you Australians were tough.' His South African accent intensified when he pronounced the *oar* in Oarstralians.

'It's not so much the weather. I just don't want to be away from home too much. And when I get home it is pitch black anyway.'

'Buy some lights. I see plenty of guys out there in Discovery Bay with lights on their helmets and on the bikes.'

The last bit hurt. I don't mind listening to a trail walker, or whatever he was, suggesting I stiffen up and ride at night, but telling me I wasn't as tough as other mid-life cyclists was like South African biltong in the belly. Hard and bitter. And he was right, which made it worse.

The wheels fell off in week three. I only managed one-hundred-and-forty kilometres due a combination of laziness and laziness. The comments piled in from my South African friend too, ranging from 'I told you, you can't count the trainer' all the way up to 'You look like you're getting fatter. Is that even possible? Maybe you should lay off the gels.' My fans clearly didn't understand the pressure cooker atmosphere of trying to complete this Le Tour monument.

Week four from the ninety week plan was even worse with only one-hundred-and-thirty completed.

I had to be honest with Neil. I sent him a mail.

Blunners, just scraped through on target this week. Have to say I'm finding it tough to get away early from work and get the miles in. I feel good about actually doing the miles but it's just finding the time. Well, when I say scraped through, I mean almost scraped through.

The first three sentences were lies of course, and the fourth was an attempt at truth to soften the lies a little bit. If I couldn't be half honest with Neil just who could I be half honest with?

To my disappointment Neil let me know in reply that he was ahead of schedule and completing almost all of his efforts out on the road where cyclists were real men. He sent me a mail:

> *I'm seeing my parents this weekend so will pick up my old tri bars to see if I can get a better average. Maybe you need to get on the hot sauce? You need a light too. Then you can go before and after work, see no problem. Surely you are getting up at 3am anyway to cycle beside the bed because of your EPO jam blood anyway.*

To rub salt in my wound Neil also let me know he bought more kit which included new shoes and lights for his bikes due to all of the night riding he was getting in. So he was a) doing the miles, b) doing them on the road, and c) doing them at night when his family were asleep, which meant my last vestige of honour in 'at least being with my family' was a fallacy.

He then followed it up two days later with more tales of training completed, even though the quality wasn't quite there.

> *Was up at 5.15 am this morning for a bike ride. I don't know why I bother, it was truly shocking. Felt like I had a hangover although I looked a million*

quid in my Bianchi World Road Race champion
colours. I even gave the bike a wax last night, felt
nice and smooth to the touch.

I didn't know you could wax a bike. Ignoring this piece however I knew something had to be done about getting the miles in. I turned it around with a cracking, up at dawn, ninety kilometres, much of it in the rain. This was a big ride for me at the time and the longest on my own. Out in the rain I convinced myself that lesser mortals like my South African trail walker friend were at home while I was out there in the field defying the raging storms. For those German or Australian cycling fans out there think Heinreich Haussler and his Tour de France stage thirteen win but a little slower and without the tears. They were miserable conditions from the forty kilometre mark but surprisingly enjoyable. I rode laps of a long straight road near the airport in Hong Kong and in the fastest section even managed to lose the back-end in a puddle. I thought I had aquaplaned but subsequent research lead me to believe bike tyres are too thin to lose all road contact due to a cushion of water unless they reach speeds of one hundred miles per hour. I just lost grip in the water somehow.

On arrival back home I felt like a conqueror returning to the village. My wench was up and pottering around the fire, or rather the kettle, as was my progeny, and I was back, chafed, worn and victorious. Later that day I even contemplated an hour on the trainer, but both my daughter and my old friend laziness demanded otherwise, so we made Dora puzzles instead.

I reeled off another fifty kilometres on the road the following morning and then forty the following week, completing the target. Five weeks down, sixty weeks to go.

It was at this point that Lucien offered some of his elder statesman counsel. He explained to Wendy over the phone that we had no chance of completing Le Tour. He thought we wouldn't have the legs. He thought two hour training rides once a week were not enough. He thought eight hour days climbing in the Alps or Pyrenees are a test for any cyclists let alone someone that doesn't know a mountain-side from a backside. He also went on to decline the generous offer of being our man in the van, as in our driver, soigneur, mechanic, guide, food and drink supplier. Lucien brushed our offer aside with a Flemish shrug which is similar to a Gallic shrug but with less effort. Apparently he thought it would be boring. I couldn't see how driving around the French country-side for three weeks at thirty kilometres an hour (or less) could be conceived as boring, especially if he was to be given a ringside seat to our transformation into giants of the road, but he is Belgian after all and maybe just wanted to be on the bike. There it was, perhaps he was jealous. The criticisms didn't end there. The logistics and practicalities were also not to be underestimated, he said. He thought we would spend most of our time looking at maps, and that we would be stopping and starting all day, losing momentum, taking the wrong turns and find ourselves on busy roads and motorways.

I told Neil of the comments the following day. Never mind, I said, it is just fuel for the fire. Lucien was just one of many nay-sayers out there. In this case nay is the Dutch word for no (spelt *nee*, pronounced 'nay'), so the title fit like a glove. Yes, he was a 'non-believer' in Texan parlance. Sure, there would be plenty like this, and they were just like any other on-road challenge to be swatted out of the way of our destiny. In response to the busy roads comment and the maps we had two words for him which went together like salt and pepper; Neil and GPS. Armed with an expensive global positioning device on the front of Neil's bike we could circumnavigate the world at the touch of a button.

Neil responded in a positive frame of mind. He said there are roads in Belgium full of flowers and butterflies and there are roads to glory. We had chosen our path. Those old school Belgians with their local knowledge and hours and hours of training were going to be given a lesson in cycling by two time-crunched cyclists with bike shop internet accounts.

CYCLING THROUGH THE DARK
(Neil)

David Millar wrote a book titled 'Racing through the Dark'. It's a pretty good read and helps elucidate why particular cyclists turn to shadowy elements of the sport. I read and re-read this book and was left with a slight sense of disappointment however because at no point does David actually physically cycle in the dark. I think that this is a fairly major aspect missing from his cycling resume, and one that separates the pros from the amateurs. Most amateurs who love riding and need to earn a living are forced out into the deep night hours at some stage.

Cycling in the dark is something that has been part of my life since my first bundle of joy arrived, and it wasn't my suggestion. I remember finally shipping my beloved Giant TCR from my parent's house three years after I had moved out. I had decided that I wanted to take up cycling again. I started with a few smaller rides of around thirty miles. Every time I got back to the house I would be confronted with one very angry looking wife, often with a vein popping alarmingly from her head, holding a screaming child. I am not suggesting that she pinched our little one in order to achieve screaming at the exact moment I walked in the door, but the timing seemed uncanny.

'Alright?'

It would be at this point that I would receive 'The Look' and for those of you who think that Lance has sole rights to 'The Look' you would be very wrong. Withering is not the word. I am a cyclist of many years so already have a somewhat withered appearance. Brutalising is perhaps a better description.

The miles started to dry up somewhat. I had suggested to Chris only weeks earlier that we ride five hundred miles a month in preparation for Le Tour, and it was going badly.

I decided to chance my arm again a few weeks later and take what I thought would be a quick jaunt out with the local cycling club, *Mellow Velo*. In a moment of weakness Laura agreed and I waved her off while she was contemplating a couple of hours of baby hell or assisted suicide.

Meanwhile I rolled up to the meeting point slightly ahead of schedule and engaged in some slightly blokey chit chat, something which I always find rather uncomfortable. It didn't matter; I would let my legs do the talking.

After some fairly tedious conversations about rear derailleurs and the outrageous price of coffee in the local café I eventually found out that there were three groups for the various abilities present; fast, medium and why-are-you-bothering is how it was pitched to me.

The fast group consisted of guys who seemingly lived, breathed and slept with their bikes on a daily basis. There was a little too much man-bike love in this group for my liking.

One of the fast guys told me that to progress in these semi-amateur ranks I needed to leave work early on Tuesdays and Thursdays and do the midweek club run as well as the Time-Trial or else I would be going no-where except 'out the backdoors'. I didn't really like to point out that in my job just popping home early two nights a week would be frowned upon and also send me out the back doors of employment.

In terms of equipment it was all Scott Addicts, Cervelos and Dura Ace with these guys and I was starting to feel inadequate. It was at this point that I thought to myself I should try the medium group.

The medium group looked about right, but there was again a very high level spec of machinery and components on show, all leaning along the wall outside.

Suddenly someone blurted out 'What the hell is that?'

Everyone turned around to look at a rather old and silver Giant TCR, which happened to be mine. I firmly believed in buying the best to look the best to be the best but at that stage couldn't afford it.

'What a piece of crap.' Cue chuckling.

I decided to distance myself as much as possible from my old clanger until the moment of departure and kept chatting.

I was told that I was more than welcome to join this group as long as I could 'effin pedal in a effin straight effin line'.

After a bit of a discussion it seemed that the medium and slow groups would set off at the same time and would be sorted in a kind of survival of the fittest, but it didn't really work out that way.

The medium crew suddenly mounted and set off. I was by now as far away from my bike as possible, with the snide bike remarks still ringing in the ears. There was no choice but to go with the slow group. There were old riders with old jerseys, young riders with brand new team kit, there were big guys with bellies over hanging lycra and two thin guys who rounded out the group. The scene reminded me a bit like a nightclub dance floor at two in the morning, i.e. the unwanted, and I slotted into the group perfectly.

We set off and were soon at a surprisingly high speed. We went straight through some red traffic lights, always a pet hate of mine and I found myself next to Barry.

Barry was in his fifties, he was wearing a garish trade shirt and ubiquitous eighties wrap-around sunglasses. Barry was obsessed with cycling and cycle racing.

Barry used to race, Barry was very effin good apparently, he told me with a wink. Barry liked to effin swear, he could have been a contender but he was in reality a bit shite, he said. Like me.

Just then the group ran over a rabbit, almost severing head from body. The peloton let out a deafening roar of approval. I was personally more interested in avoiding the poor bunny and Barry's sudden swerve to get into the spirit.

The peloton shuffled around a bit and I found myself riding with Martin. Martin didn't like to hug the kerb so I found myself either half a foot wider than everyone else on the wrong side of the road or clashing bars with him to stay in line. Martin was a bit portly, but had a decent turn of speed until his lungs stopped matching his legs.

We chatted amicably about quite a few topics and despite initial reservations Martin turned out to be a very nice guy. The conversation then changed to jobs and Martin mentioned that he ran an insurance company. I smiled weakly. I knew he would ask me what I did for a living and I would have to tell him I had a very boring job in a very large back office in a very large bank.

I told Larry I was a pilot. I have no idea why I did that. I am not sure whether I was forcing myself out of the peloton through lies, or enjoying being a fool in the freedom of strangers but the words came out and I couldn't put them back in.

The peloton carved its way through various villages I had never heard of until I found myself in the second row of the group next to a character on a green Bianchi called Quentin. Closer inspection revealed that Quentin's bike wasn't all that it seemed as he 'only' had a Veloce groupset, which although costing about the same as my entire bike was still second choice for the Bianchi crowd.

Within minutes we were both positioned at the front of the group until a set of traffic lights ground us to a halt. Obviously I didn't know which way to go so I asked my new companion who somewhat forcefully told me that we were to turn left. I slowly turned my head left to see that we were to be climbing a slight hill for the next few kilometres, which suited me. I fancied myself as a climber.

When you ride with a new club there is often some sort of race to determine who the alpha male is, especially if you are approaching your mid-life years. This process was about to begin with Quentin.

The lights changed and we all clicked in and turned for the hill. Immediately Quentin started to half wheel me or edge just in front, very poor cycling etiquette, akin to blowing the contents of your nose on to the rider behind. I noticed that Quentin pedalled very much like Lance, he was turning his legs faster than a Zanussi on spin cycle and continued to half wheel me.

The race was on, me against him, beta male versus beta male. That fragile little male ego of mine came to the fore. I decided to get the small hammer out. Instead of my being half wheeled it was now him. I changed the small hammer for a medium weight claw and cranked the pace up another notch, clicking into a higher gear. Quentin responded by lowering his head and making a rasping noise, legs still whizzing round like a Catherine wheel. Just as I was about to pull out the sledge hammer to blow him away I heard a few shouts.

'Oi oi slow it down, we are losing people.'

I turned around to see a fractured group. I would have smiled to myself except I was struggling to think straight in the oxygen debt I was slowly dying from. I hadn't ridden any longer than an hour or so on my recent solo rides and we were now up to two hours and hadn't even reached our halfway destination. I was left to fend for myself on the front for the next twenty minutes battling against the sea winds while Quentin seemed to be dying silently beside me. Luckily some of the stronger riders then took over the front and we wafted into the seaside town. This is where the first of many heated discussions began.

It became immediately obvious that the slow group liked to find a grotty café for something to eat and drink before heading home. This created a standoff split in the group where five of the guys decided they wouldn't set foot in the chosen café. A lively debated ensued while the merits of each establishment were assessed. The choice of tea leaves and instant coffee, the benefits of what type of cake was sold and naturally the price were all thrown into the mix but eventually the choice seemed to boil down to one thing. Which establishment had the fittest waitress?

The matter was settled and everyone entered the café. The dissenters threw their gear in the corner and set about sulking and muttering for the next hour over the choice of café, especially 'Mr Cervelo'

'Dave, I told you Dave, the tea in here is two bob mate.'

'I know mate, but what are we gonna do?'

'I don't wanna leave me bike outside mate, someone will nick it.'

There was no chance of anyone nicking my bike unfortunately.

The café was quite possibly the darkest and most unhygienic looking eating establishment in Britain but staggeringly at least eight giants of the road ordered the full heart-attack-inducing English fried breakfast. I picked a small table with three other guys and ordered a cup of hot chocolate.

What followed was a deathly slow break of close to an hour. Half of the group were happy to sloth around and eat for their lives while the other half groaned about the time it was taking. I kept my mouth shut. No-one wanted to hear from the new chump and I was unsure as to which group I wished to align myself. My heart was with the whingers naturally. I agreed, how could it take anyone this long to have a drink and a snack? Talk turned to cycling kit and comments were made about my rather expensive attire. I smiled weakly and lied, saying they were all presents. I also agreed that all bankers should be hung, drawn and quartered. Luckily I didn't have to discuss my piloting skills as no-one asked this again. The group then discussed bikes at length. Luckily for me no-one mentioned the thirteen year old Giant that looked fit for the scrap heap.

I phoned Laura who was not at all pleased to hear that my two hour ride had now taken three hours and I was still nowhere near home.

Finally the group was underway again. I would like to say we 'roared home' but it was more of a squeak due to arthritic joints and the additional comfort break forced through middle-aged prostate issues.

I found myself at the back until the first hill loomed into view. The guy directly in front of me nipped off to the head of the group and kept going off up the hill, bouncing around in his saddle like Contador. I sprinted after him and again the group fractured. I was on the wheel of the oldest looking guy in the group and I thought about going around him when suddenly my legs didn't feel quite so special any more and my lungs began to heave with the exertion.

I then realised with horror that my current form was perhaps better aligned with this slow group than any other. I would need to train hard to even scrape into the bottom of the medium group. I stuck to his wheel until the summit. It wasn't long after this that we had to climb another long hill before we turned right across a lane of moving traffic.

Mr Cervelo, still smarting from the choice of cafe, took his frustrations out on a passing car. Almost without warning he decided that the car had passed too close to his riding partner, Mrs. Cervelo, and he was going to punch the window as hard as he possibly could, twice, whilst simultaneously shouting the word 'wanker'.

The young lad in the passenger seat almost had a soiled trouser moment with shock, as did I. The car driver then pulled down his window and started shouting obscenities in return. He madly revved his engine and attempted to lurch his car forward to clip Mr Cervelo.

Mr Cervelo responded by kicking the car as hard as he could. The driver responded with blue smoke from his burning clutch. Mr Cervelo then rode to the front of the green fiat Punto and stood there, glaring. The driver decided that enough was enough and jumped out of his door to confront his nemesis. Within seconds though he was surrounded by what looked like a scene out of *Cocoon* as the elderly cyclists from the group shuffled over in their cleated shoes to threaten assault while the younger ones looked on.

I positioned myself around the corner, cowardly avoiding all confrontation whilst pretending to look at the time on my watch.

More obscenities from both sides continued for another minute or so until both parties resumed their positions at steering wheels and handle bars and rode off. Ten minutes later we were back at our starting point and I turned off alone toward my house. The relief was palpable when I clicked my heels out of the bike. There's no place like home.

I say that, but then Laura remonstrated with me for twenty minutes on the merits of sticking to my word in terms of time away from home. She was right. I was wrong. I agreed wholeheartedly and said I would never do it again.

On reflection there were a lot of good guys on the ride but it was not for me. It is not always easy to get a perfect match between my own biking needs and that of a club. Each individual has a slightly different view of hours, speed, distance, breaks, etiquette and violence toward motorists. In isolation one can learn to adapt but collectively the differences were never going to work for me, particularly with young children and a determined Laura. This was actually the last time I ever joined a club ride. The events on the continent with the old Flemish masters and Chris are the closest I have come to riding in a peloton since. I knew I had to start looking at other ways in which I could cycle the hours whilst avoiding a messy and expensive divorce.

This is where cycling in the dark took hold. Various cycling magazines had interesting articles on night riding which at the time seemed the only logical way that I could continue getting the miles in. What would I need for riding at night? Well lights obviously, but I almost had a mild coronary when I saw the price, especially for quality front lights. I wasn't sure I was going to be able to buy the best to look the best but as it was night time my appearance was less important. In total I spent a couple of hundred pounds on lights and high visibility garments. I had to make it count.

Two days after the lights arrived I set off on my first night ride. Being a night rider might be fun for the Hoff but from the start I could see we were going to have to overcome a few challenges. I hit my first pothole within three hundred metres of home. Crunch. I knew it was there, I had ridden around it about two hundred times in the past, but at night while concentrating on everything else I missed it cold. Crunch. I hit a second one about a mile further down the road. Again this was a hole I was used to so I was as frustrated with myself as I was with the local council's lunar landscape. Luckily I hadn't punctured. I continued on, and noted solemnly that I was cycling slower than usual.

Aside from avoiding holes in the ground the night riding experience introduced a new level of vulnerability and fear of making new holes in my body or my expensive new night riding and polar air busting kit. Each time a set of car lights began to creep up I would tense the shoulders slightly and prepare for impact. As the car passed I would breathe a short sigh of relief and resume riding with my owl-like eyes open as wide as possible.

I returned home after almost an hour and a half, having ridden only twenty five miles. I sent a lie to Chris via email telling him that he should get out and ride at night as it was a great way to get the miles in. If I should endure the fear of racing through the dark why shouldn't he. I knew he was also getting his miles done on a stationary bike, hardly the best way to train. After three more night rides of my own I think he had a point.

Most cyclists find stationary bikes and trainers loathsome. When cycling on the road the air rushes over you and cools you down. On a trainer there is no air so you are dripping with sweat after only a few minutes. Additionally the boredom is as stifling as the heat. Due to the noise, Laura would never let me ride the thing in the house so I let it rot in the conservatory. The mere sight of the thing sends me into a state of uncontrolled anxiety but I had to do it. The club ride had been shelved, the night riding was also in danger of consignment and I had no other choice but to dust off the turbo trainer.

ZEELAND PREPARATION
(Chris)

The planned trip to Belgium was only a few months away. I suggested to Neil via email that he come too and we go for a long ride with Lucien and his friends and put down a marker. The nay sayers had to be converted to ja sayers.

Neil tentatively agreed and said he would run the idea past his wife who I should say appears to wear the lycra pants in their family. He responded a couple of days later with a resounding yes, having struck some sort of deal which involved painting and decorating for months on end in the dark with no supper. Neil sent a mail.

I'm in. They are going to cream us. Training for six weeks is not going to cut it against those guys so forget that. I'm just going to have to buy more gear. Then we will smash them.

Neil was right. You had to look the best to be the best. We then spent at least an hour a day for the following month researching and agreeing the kit. We went for the black ASSOS short sleeved full-zipped jersey which meant black shorts, black shades, black shoes, world championship socks and black gloves. We were going to look ridiculous.

Lucien came back with a course that took in close to one hundred and sixty kilometres of Belgium and Holland, including the Zeelandbrug in Holland which featured in the 2010 Tour De France. I asked for a map but instead got a list of villages. I had forgotten that Belgians do not do maps.

Essen

Essen - Hoek

Huybergen

Hoogerheide

Woensdrecht

Oesterdam

via het eiland Tholen naar de Philipsdam

Bruinisse

Ouwerkerk

Zierikzee met stop in café De Gekroonde Suikerbiet

Zeelandbrug

richting Goes

Wilhelminadorp

Kattendijke

Wemeldingen

Yerzeke met stop in de haven

Oostdijk

Gaweege

naast de Westerschelde naar Bath

Ossendrecht

Huybergen

Essen - Hoek met als afsluiter De Bostella (cafe)

Essen

It was going to be my longest ride ever, and my first with Neil. When told of the newcomer to his peloton, Lucien asked: 'This Englishman, he can ride can't he? And you too? It's a long way.' What a question. We needed to prove to him that yes, we can ride. Yes, we can become giants of the road. Yes, we will do the tour. Yes, possibly with the use of enhancements. In response I should have quoted the great man from Texas and said that more people should believe in us as athletes and believe in miracles. I said we would be fine.

One massive challenge for Neil was going to be transportation of his bike. Obsessive is a word which underplays Neil's devotion to the paintwork, let alone the mechanics, and he was loathe to let his brand new Boardman be tossed about by baggage handlers on the train. He quickly realised that unless he bought a hard bike carrier and was happy to let the bike disappear out of his sight and into a luggage hold he was going to have to settle for something else.

I mentioned it to Lucien and he told me not to worry, it was Belgium, and we would find a loaner bike for the day.

A few days later Lucien sent me a mail with a photo of potential bike for the ride.

Hier een foto van twee fietsen die bij mij staan en welke we mogen gebruiken voor de rit. Groetjes uit Essen

I forwarded it on to Neil without looking at the photo but could tell from the response the bike didn't quite match lofty expectations.

Oh my, a piece of history...marvellous! I could be in trouble with down-shifters and only five gears. Still, I need to fit in....I need to live and breathe the beautiful Belgian air, the spiritual home of cycling, soak up the beauty, tame the pave, be a part of history, ride a bike from history.

The bike looked in great condition mechanically but had a vintage 1980s aura about it and came complete with a massive leather saddle. A new email from Belgium quickly followed which included a photograph of a similar looking model from Diamant, though this bike at least had drop handle bars.

I asked Lucien for something built in the last ten years. Clearly no-one was going to part with their carbon Cannondale for the day but he assured me that there would be something more modern to hand. We wondered whether this was an attempt to hobble the foreigners.

One week out from the big event we patiently waited for more news. For an average cyclist like me the style and quality of bike is a big deal, but for Neil 'Buy the Best' Blundell it is a matter of great consequence, and possibly the greatest. I wondered why he refused to bring one of his lesser bikes to the party, something aluminium perhaps. Surely the damage on the train would be minimal if the bike is stored in a hard case. I put the question to Neil on three occasions but he refused. He had a thing about trains which seemingly outweighed his thing about riding the best and he insisted we go with a borrowed bicycle.

It was shortly after the latest refusal from Neil that the penny dropped. It was part of the plan. Obviously by borrowing someone else's ill-fitting old and third-hand bike Neil would be able prove just how incredibly adaptable he was. Lucien knew that Neil adjusted his saddle and waxed his bike before sleep. I had told him. I also explained that he bought the best to beat the best. So Neil was subtly telling me and the Belgians; 'Any port in a storm *there in Belgium* old boy. I can take some old rusty lump of a bike that you throw at me and still be a giant of the road. I am British.'

Additionally, and I am sure the thought only came to me rather than Neil at least at a conscious level, if he failed miserably Neil had a get-out clause: The bike was rubbish. Brilliant. It took the best brain to beat the best too and that can't be bought. I imagined him bursting into *Land of Hope and Glory* as we took off on the ride.

Neil would soon learn however that cycling in Belgium is the peloton of hard knocks. They cannot be out-foxed. Don't even try. They had been there and done that and seen all the tricks and if they could be bothered getting off their bikes long enough they would write a book about it. Neil was shocked by the offer that was shortly to come.

BROKEN BONES AND MOBILE PHONES
(Neil)

Soon after Chris said he was training seriously on a road bike he suggested we meet up and go for a long ride in Belgium. I realised with horror that I needed to get back out on the road and fast. Aside from buying kit I had done little else other than tell Chris I used to be good. More training was required.

The night rides, club rides and turbo trainer rides were consigned to history so the old fashioned training style of solo day rides needed to be added to my shrinking repertoire. This meant business now. I couldn't face the prospect of humiliation at the hands of my apprentice. I should say I do like to think of Chris in terms of being an apprentice or rather, my protégé. Most Australians are good on a bike but usually end up on the wrong side of the podium. I told Chris he was the best lead-out middle-aged man in lycra in the world but he should let me look after the finish line. Like all good domestiques Chris took this in good spirits. He knew that I had a history in the sport rather than taking it up in my twilight years, and he also knew he was a bit heavy at eighty-eight kilos.

Aside from my competitive nature taking over I also wanted to prevent Chris from finding out the awful truth, which was that a handful of club rides spread out over ten years and one Etape does not a cyclist make. I was only moderately better than Chris I suppose, but didn't want him to know his team leader was a sporting fraud.

Thus I needed to continue the lie, but quietly. I had to slowly and secretly drag myself into the kind of physical shape that could back up my words with actions.

At that time the garage housed my two road bikes. There was one bike for summer and one for inclement winter weather. The first ride out of my cycling dormancy did not deserve the good bike, so winter it was. I wiped the cobwebs and live insects away, pumped the fully deflated tyres back to life and contemplated riding early the next day.

I opened the walk-in cycling wardrobe door and went to the winter section, carefully removing the various thick cold-weather garments that would keep me warm and snug. One particular favourite was my wind-stopper bib-tights which were bought soon after a touch of frost nip visited a delicate area.

The first ride, after a hiatus of almost half a year, was a sorry affair. I was passed on a couple of occasions and cut a ride short on another, but slowly and surely the mileage began to tally. I felt like I was emerging from a six-year hibernation rather than six months, but slowly the warmth began to spread to my legs. I told Chris that the Eagle of Dartford would again soar over the Kentish lowlands.

A series of snowstorms across the United Kingdom, however, meant that soaring opportunities were put on hold. The local routes were covered in a good few inches of snow and were fairly un-roadworthy for someone of limited bike handling ability. Three weeks went by without a ride and my fitness levels were retreating.

I trawled the internet, trying to find ways of gaining fitness without effort. One article I found stated that in a grand tour a cyclist's haematocrit levels, or oxygen-rich red blood cell levels, shrank due to the effects of fatigue. This article, and it's seemingly innocuous assertions, encouraged me to think that in order to keep my red blood cells at optimum levels I should stay away from training.

I mentioned this plan to Chris who was surprised at my training schedule. He was still under the illusion that you actually needed to train hard to get fitter. I told him he needed to believe in miracles and buy better gear.

While I was resting up and gaining even more strength there was a nagging doubt that at some point I would have to get out on the bike again. The thought hardly made me leap with joy. The snow was starting to thin on the ground though and the bike once again began to call me. I would have to mount the steed again.

I set out early the next morning. It was bitterly cold and dark and within minutes my hands were beginning to numb from the arctic conditions. My ears and face quickly followed suit and in all it was becoming a rather interesting experience. I was moaning and cursing. I think there are two types of cyclists; those who are natural optimists and only see the positive in every mishap that comes their way, and the cynics who believe every rotten piece of weather or broken component has happened for the sole reason to annoy. I obviously fall into the latter category.

Trying to stick to the planned eating and hydration levels I reached down for my water bottle and took a swig. Nothing. I tried again and discovered that the bottle had frozen solid. I thought of the sunny climate that Chris was probably riding in and an overwhelming sense of jealousy swept through my whole being. This really wasn't fair. My domestique was ready to take over.

I did what any fair weather cyclist would do in my position. I gave up, turned around and went home. I packed.

Later the same day it began to snow again. Not the little fluffy kind that you see in Hollywood movies but huge snowflakes that covered the garden in minutes. Within hours over two inches of snow had fallen and any thought of my earlier miserable episode were safely consigned to some recess in my brain.

The snow eventually began to clear later in the week, along with a slow and gradual rise in temperature. Laura had already determined earlier in the week that the weekend cycle would be postponed due to adverse weather conditions. She looked out of the window and gave me a look of feigned disappointment. I had other ideas on the matter and had no choice but to train.

On Saturday morning I woke early and carefully selected each item of biking attire to make absolutely certain I was North Pole proof. I put on a windproof face mask that gave me the appearance of some kind of revolutionary activist but it cut the wind chill from my face. I had to forego the whole 'looking the best' mantra.

In short I looked completely ridiculous but I was determined to get a decent ride in, my reputation as patron of our peloton of two depended on it.

I began my ride and was pleasantly surprised with how this meticulous planning and attention to clothing detail had paid off. I was neither too hot nor too cold and instead was wedged firmly in cycling Nirvana.

I followed my usual route which took in one busy main road before turning off into a series of quiet country lanes, travelling further and further away from civilisation. At this point in the ride, while off the main roads and meandering along some quiet picturesque countryside, I started to relax and enjoy the cycling.

Like most cyclists I use this time for thinking about various problems or issues I have. There are no interruptions. The clarity of thought you can achieve during a long ride knows no bounds. But there are times also when my mind begins to wander. I often daydream of breaking away in a tour stage, crowds lining the roads, chanting my name as I increase my lead on a frustrated peloton.

Forty five minutes had passed and I was in full dream mode, happily tapping out a reasonable thirty kilometres per hour in the freezing weather. Hardly breakaway pace really but it was a dream after all.

Suddenly something roused me from my cycling induced stupor. I glimpsed some snow at the side of the road whilst climbing up a particularly remote section. I then spotted some tell-tale signs of ice on the road which I knew could be fairly catastrophic on a road bike. The only good advice for cycling on icy roads is not to. I decided to continue around the corner and turn around in the next available lay by. There was no point taking risks. As Andy Schlek would say after a particularly wet or downhill stage: 'We all have families to go home to.'

Bang.

There was a sickening thud, followed instantly by agonising pain in the area of my right hip.

My next sight was of tarmac barrelling towards me at eye level as I slid gracefully up the hill, with my bike skidding slightly in front of me. I came to a stop, but my beloved bike continued arcing towards the centre of the road.

Usually in situations like this I would try to jump straight up, generally due to the embarrassment of crashing in front of a bus load of people while trying to unclip my cleats.

This time however when I tried to move I realised that my right leg didn't want to play ball. I struggled to put weight on it, but quickly realised it would be a futile exercise.

The pain was now making me feel nauseous. I hopped over to my bike, with pain shooting up my leg and back, and I gingerly picked it up and dragged it to the side of the road by a small grass verge. I didn't sit down as I couldn't bend my leg. I fished around in my pockets for the phone, wondering how I was going to tell

Laura the embarrassing situation I was in. With a sense of rising dread I realised that I hadn't taken my mobile phone with me. Excellent.

Panic slowly started to spread. I was stuck in the middle of nowhere with a best case scenario being a badly bruised hip, and worst case scenario an amputation. I was at least fifteen miles from home.

I turned to my right to see two road cyclists coming towards me, my salvation.

'Watch out guys,' I said, 'there are some patches of ice up ahead. I've just come off.'

'Are you ok?'

'Yeah course, I'm fine.'

And with that they were gone. To this day, I still don't know what was going through my mind. I needed medical help and yet I sent them on their way rather than borrowing a phone. I think it is a man thing, or at least a British man thing. We don't ask for directions or help. This especially applies to me when I am woken from a splendid day-dream in which I was bursting through the pain barrier to claim cycling glory over a peloton.

So I had chosen my path. I would be making my own way home somehow with only one working leg. I would like to chronicle the return home as a portrait of a man who knows no barrier to pain, a man who can suffer like no other, a man who knows no fear. Regrettably though, that would be a lie.

Quickly examining my fallen bike I noticed that fortunately the damage seemed to be restricted to my leg and my pride. A small piece of silver plastic had shattered on the top of the hood exposing the rusting mechanical underbelly, but other than that it remained relatively unscathed.

This was only second time I had worn my Gore Oxygen jacket. Next step before looking at the damage to my now shaking leg was to desperately examine the shoulder and elbow region of the jacket, making sure there weren't any holes. Damn, there was an oily mark to the cuff. Pony.

I changed my mind about the leg. There was no need to look, I knew it was wrecked. I tried to get back on the bike which was problematic as I couldn't put any pressure whatsoever on my right leg. I was starting to feel the cold now and knew I had to mount somehow.

Concocting various plans in my head I set about getting back on at all costs. Every attempt gave way to an agonising torture and a groan. Finally I managed to get the bike at such an angle where I could position my right leg over the frame without bending it. This whole procedure introduced my back into the pain party. Prior to then I thought the back was fine, now it was sending sharp signals.

Once positioned over the bike-frame I had to somehow get my foot clipped into the pedal. I momentarily wished I had cheap and easy flat pedals, and cursed my innate need to buy the best. Perched on the saddle I decided to free wheel down the hill. Instinct took over eventually and I clipped in my left foot.

Leaving my right leg dangling in mid-air both hurt, and made my cycling line fairly erratic, so I gingerly placed my right foot on the pedal and began pedalling with my left foot in isolation. The pain was excruciating.

There were fifteen miles to go. My thoughts started uncontrollably changing from one subject to another. Perhaps I should get off and flag down a motorist. A flash of yellow went past. The only car I had seen since the crash.

The cycling hallucinations and delusions of grandeur also started in earnest but this time rather than launching a heroic breakaway from the peloton I imagined myself in a test of broken man against the pitiless elements. I considered, quite seriously, what Captain Scott would have done in this position. He would have rallied his men and carried on regardless with grim determination. He wouldn't have asked for a lift home in a yellow Renault. I guess it wasn't exactly the South Pole and I was hardly Neil of the Kent-Arctic.

I was woken from my dream when a junction loomed menacingly into view. In my state it looked like Mont Ventoux. I approached by unclipping my foot and coasting at about five miles per hour toward the end of the road. I briefly lost balance and righted myself instantly before coming to a neat stop. A second fall would have been unthinkable.

I waited at the junction, unsure of where to turn. Going left would have been the usual route. It was slightly shorter but with some stinging hills. Right was longer but had only one steep-ish hill and then some rolling terrain back to my house. I clipped in with my able foot and turned right onto the main road, flicking up through the gears toward a major roundabout.

Fortunately there was little traffic and I continued up towards the main hill without slowing. I had travelled over five miles now. If cycling is truly about suffering I decided I was due a place in the Jens Voigt hall of pain.

I changed down into the granny ring to find myself pedalling the proverbial 'squares', with a shocking stop-and-start rotation. I was cursing my lack of a compact chain-set and matching girl's edition cassette. Common practise for serious cyclists these days is to practise pedalling with only one leg, to strengthen various muscles and improve technique. I had never contemplated this however and could see my stroke was full of dead-spots. In the cycle of my leg, from one o'clock until six o'clock everything was fine but anything past six was a grimace and a growl. I had gleaned from cycling magazines that the best way to pedal is pretend you are scraping dog poo from your shoe to clear the dead spot and now I was scraping bucket-full's.

The hill seemed to grow longer. I almost began the cycling equivalent of sailing's tacking, or zigzagging across the road to reduce the gradient, but my cycling pride wouldn't allow it. A climb that I would normally power over in the big ring was now almost reducing me to a standstill. Soon though I reached the summit. Thank you. I blew the air out of my lungs at the relief. I free-wheeled, catching my breath as I began to pick up speed down the other side. There were only a few small inclines left, ten minutes maximum.

If another cyclist had overtaken me at this point I think I would have got off the bike and cried.

The next ten minutes passed in a confusing blur of pain, immense personal courage and faux Germanic shouts in my head of 'shut up legs'. I finally turned into my road and sluggishly wheeled past the front window to the house, desperately trying to find Laura who didn't appear to be around. After gingerly dismounting I made my way into the back garden and caught a glimpse of myself in the window. The reflection looked too good and was not that of someone who had just had a huge crash, I had hoped for a more pitiful appearance.

I tapped on the window and after what seemed like an eternity Laura appeared at the back door, with a look of ever so slight concern on her face.

'What's happened' she asked

'I fell off on the ice, my hip really hurts. Can you help me in?' I replied.

Laura has a medical background and she quickly examined me.

'We have to take you to hospital. Now.'

'No it's ok, I'll just rest it a bit, put on some ice.'

'Er no, you are going to the hospital to be checked out.'

'I can't, its Olivia's birthday, I have to go to that.'

'Neil. I think you have fractured your leg, you aren't going anywhere other than the emergency room.'

Ten minutes later with almost military efficiency Laura had both me and our eighteen month-old daughter packed up and ready to go. Admittedly I was being fairly pathetic but I would like to point out that firstly my body seemed to be stiffening very quickly and secondly, well I actually am pretty pathetic.

By the time we arrived at the hospital my leg was so painful that I couldn't move it at all. Laura said that she would go and get some help for me so I sat in the car and waited. And waited, and waited.

I started daydreaming again. What would Chris Boardman be doing in a situation like this? Well Chris was used to crashing and breaking things. He most probably had an 'accident bag' that he kept safely at home that his wife picked up every time the weekly hospital call came. I should obtain a good quality bag for the future and buy the best in order to recover the best.

After what seemed like an eternity Laura appeared into view. Hmmm, she seemed to be on her own. The consultant must have been just behind her ferrying his crack team of athlete specialists to work on the fallen hero.

I looked more closely and realised it was just Laura and she was pushing a wheelchair.

'Effing hell, you have got to be kidding me.'

'What?'

'I'm not getting in that. Can't you get me a stretcher or something?'

I then received 'The Look'.

Laura quite firmly told me to get my skinny arse into the chair and stop being a 'whining brat'.

I complied.

She wheeled me into the accident and emergency ward, parking me next to a poor old lady with dried blood on her face who was evidently another unsuspecting victim of the deadly black ice.

With my suspected broken leg I imagined somewhat naively that I might be seen before the drunken teenager sporting a cut lip.

Oh, how wrong could I be?

Three hours later I was wheeled into a bay where my particulars were taken. I was lifted onto the bed and asked to move my leg which proved impossible. I was told that due to my age and general fitness, it was unlikely I had broken my leg.

I let out an anguished cry.

'Noooo.'

'Doctor, surely I have broken it?'

'How fast were going.'

'Er about twenty-three kilometres per hour.'

With the doctor being British this obviously meant nothing to him. He gave me some painkillers and I was left for twenty minutes.

When he returned I could now slightly bend my leg, at which point the doctor said I could go home, it was just badly bruised.

'But I can't move,' I replied.

'Let me help you.' He then swung my legs around and watched me. I couldn't put any weight on my leg.

'Maybe you should have some crutches.'

'Do you think!?'

He re-appeared with a set of crutches and was about to disappear until I asked him how on earth to use them.

He obviously had somewhere better to be as I received a ten second demonstration.

I hobbled to the reception. Laura by now had gone home to feed my daughter. My misery complete, I ordered a cab home.

Weeks passed and I still couldn't bear any weight on my leg to walk but strangely I could go on the turbo trainer. A second opinion confirmed what I knew all along.

I had a hairline fracture. Victory!

I was there and then officially inducted into the cycling Hall of Pain.

Within seven months I would have to ride a one-hundred-and-sixty kilometre Belgium epic on a recently 'broken' leg. Heroic.

CONTINENTAL RIFT
(Chris)

In the meantime there was the matter of Lucien's invitation to the Sunday ride with his club, *'t Pedalleke*. The details of the ride were explained to me in Flemish. Unfortunately, my knowledge of Flemish is somewhere between child-like and basic, so I misunderstood most of it. How important could the details be though? I understood 'club, twenty people, seventy kilometres, and fast at the end.' That was enough.

'Sounds great.' I told him. I added that I would happily sit at the back and stay out of everyone's way. I was in great shape and I could ride for hours. This was different to previous visits to Belgium. No longer was I the Crocodile Dundee fish-out of-water first time cyclist in baggy shorts. I could change a tyre in less than ten minutes. I had lycra.

The ride started off brilliantly. The day was perfect for cycling. Bright, clear and still. We were riding through the Belgian countryside on impossibly flat roads, through cornfields and cow paddocks with rabbits and chickens scurrying out of the peloton's way. It was absolute picture book terrain and the legs were tip-top to boot. I was floating on air, absolutely loving the cycling and the holiday. Added to this, one of the cyclists who I had met before commented that I looked like a cyclist now. My awesome thighs must have caught his well-trained eye. I wondered whether the day could get any better.

The kilometres were rolling along and I was chatting away in the heart of peloton, enjoying my status as the token celebrity Australian while casually answering the key national questions. Yes, everyone knows Robbie McEwen and he is very famous (this is not quite true). No, Cadel Evans is not 'a Janette, he is married'.

After fifty kilometres Lucien pulled alongside and told me in Flemish, in the pieces I understood anyway:

'This is what I was saying yesterday, at the end we will go very quickly and you can do what you want.'

That was how I translated it in my head. I can't be sure what he actually said verbatim. I especially couldn't work out what he meant by doing 'what I want'. A wheelie perhaps? Ride no-hands? Or go somewhere else? I was in the middle of nowhere without a map and was unlikely to disappear up the road or take a stream of consciousness artistic left turn. I stayed where I was and kept riding.

At seventy kilometres we were riding alongside a river on a beautiful flat and wide stretch of road. I watched Lucien pull out from the front and slide back towards me in the middle of the group. As he did this the pace of the group began to quicken and I changed down through the gears, working harder to hold my position. He drew up alongside me.

'This is it Chris.'

'What?'

'Now, we go fast, you do what you want.'

'OK,' I said and wondered what he meant. I was already 'going fast', and certainly faster than a few minutes ago. We all were.

I changed down another gear, there weren't many left, and moved forward through the group as best I could. We tore through two roundabouts in succession and I watched in slight confusion as the guys ahead of me pounded away at an effort at least fifty percent harder than what they were doing only minutes before. At that stage I was happy to hang on and wondered whether the guys behind would be dropped, or whether in fact I was in their way. We reached the bottom of a hill, there were about a dozen riders ahead of me, all out of the saddle and it finally dawned; there was some sort of race to the top.

I climbed out of the saddle and hammered away at the pedals for the last few hundred metres, passing a handful of the guys on my way to the epic Belgian summit which would have been a towering fifty metres above sea level at least.

We got to the brow of the hill in a single file and rode to a stop, waiting for the others. A youngster of about eighteen, who I note had sat at the back for most of the ride, was the eventual 'winner'. The guy who had commented so positively on my new cycling look, only hours earlier, told Lucien that I was 'geen Cadel Evans' with a wink. Geen means no. What a bastard. The shame. This guy did finish behind me I should add.

This was without doubt, at least in my mind, a clear demonstration of the fabled Flemish guile that many pro cyclists talk about. Their cunning has no bounds. Pro cyclists, and mid-life crisis wannabes, do not land in Belgium and win races. They learn brutal lessons. They learn tactics. There are books from American pros devoted to their early careers riding in Belgium and Holland and the cruel learning experience that this provided as all sorts of tricks are pulled. I had similarly been planted firmly on my backside. The sprint to the finish was explained away as 'going fast at the end'. That was it. What was wrong with telling me it was a race? The result was a woeful loss and confirmation to all that I was 'no Cadel Evans'. I had been kept in the dark, rotting at the back of the peloton until the Belgian horses had bolted and then been told to giddy up.

I stood next to my bike afterwards on that lofty peak, swigging water and pulling the pieces together. I vowed to repeat the ride again armed with the knowledge that there is a finish line, it is a competition, and national pride is at stake.

On reflection one could argue that my poor understanding of Flemish, combined with a habit of nodding and saying 'ja' even when I have no clue what has been said may have contributed to my average showing. When I replay the scene over in my mind however, as I have done many times, I say 'no' to that. My Flemish was good enough, and especially good enough to hear that I was no Cadel Evans.

A FISTFUL OF BELGIANS
(Chris)

I planned to meet Neil's train at Antwerp station the afternoon before the Flemish showdown. It had been seven years since we had seen each other. Seven years of a friendship kept together through a shared passion for cycling. There were countless emails during these seven years discussing the weekend rides and the latest gear, our plans to emulate Tim Moore across the continent, new jerseys, new bikes, gears and components as well as chatting about the pro tour, Lance accusations and the latest Australian and British victories in Europe. In spite of all this correspondence and the occasional phone call I wasn't quite sure what to expect.

I had seen a few recent photos of Neil and it looked as though he hadn't changed much but I still was slightly concerned that I wouldn't recognise him. Via email he claimed he had lost some hair on his head and found it growing on his legs but in the photos I saw with helmets and sunglasses on he looked the same athletic gift to women and bike shops as he did all those years ago. Incidentally Neil claims he was asked by his wife why he wanted her to take his photo in full cycling gear to send to a mate in Australia. I take it the slight blur was caused by the shaking of her head. She accused him of a having a 'bromance'. Our thing is not a bromance, more a meeting of minds. My Aussie mates that I see regularly are big fans of Football, Rugby League, Aussie Rules, Rugby Union, Cricket, Cars, Horse Racing, you name it, but have zero in cycling. The only questions I get asked are 'have you bought more lycra?' and 'what colour lycra do you have?' which is generally followed by sniggering.

Essentially I have kept this correspondence going with Neil because he is the only person I know who likes cycling as much as I do without being a weird fanatic.

Neil did a splendid job of keeping his emotions in check when he finally alighted from the train. He resisted the urge to give me a massive bear hug and tell me he missed me and instead there was a very manly and masculine handshake under the majestic Antwerpen Centraal Station clock.

Getting immediately down to business Neil showed me his bag full of gels, miracle powders and protein bars apparently 'endorsed by the Hog'.

Neil is a believer in outspending your fellow cyclist. It's 'the one percent-ers'. On seeing the Olympics and Tour De France this year I would consider this a very British trait and one that has proved extremely successful. That mantra of Neil's: 'You have to buy the best, to look the best, to be the best' was clearly evident in the multiple kit bags Neil brought to Belgium.

There was seemingly no limit to Neil's supply of cycling paraphernalia. As with most cyclists he is fixated with weight. He has carbon everything, as most serious cyclists would, such as bikes, wheels, pedals. He carries compressed air cartridges rather than a pump, and has feather-weight bottle cages and shoes. He even talked about drilling holes in his bike frames back home. A light bike is a fast bike for most people and Neil especially. I think half of Neil's obsession with relieving himself every five minutes on the bike is to immediately discard that nasty, heavy and unused liquid that made its way to the bladder, like ballast.

And when he has out spent his competitors Neil then ensures they are out-eaten. He has NASA-approved power generating gels, complex long chain carbohydrate bars and beetroot juice extract which has some sort of natural EPO quality. You have to eat the best to be the best. There is also a rigid and ordered dietary plan which must be followed to the letter. These foil wrapped fruits from the cycling gods are not to be eaten haphazardly.

And then to finish off those who dare to cross cycle paths with Neil he out-smarts them. Phone applications and devices measure power output, gradient and gear ratios. Photo-chromic sun glasses complete the picture.

Against regular cyclists Neil clearly would have turned each one per cent gain into a ten per cent improvement overall. The Belgians however were irregular. They were from an era long forgotten. They hardly use helmets. A bandana was the best you could expect. They don't wear sunglasses. They don't take water unless it rains and accidentally lands on their lips. They have kept cycling deeply rooted to its minimalist beginnings of man and bike.

Being cheap I was in the middle somewhere. I couldn't afford to buy a Blundell bling bike and instead had an aluminium tank with carbon forks. I had decent shoes, shirts and glasses but ultimately looked like I had made half an effort for the ball, wearing a tuxedo on top of a pair of speedos. Having a crap bike, the crappiest in our little peloton, was going to be embarrassing.

All the talk up to this point had been about boys vs. men, and the pretenders vs. the veterans. Aside from Lucien there were to be four other Flemish cyclists joining us. They were all over sixty.

Neil and I made our way back to Essen on the train. Lucien promised that there would be a bike for Neil waiting for us when we arrived at the house. We had kindly declined the generous offer of the 1980s Merckx and the 1983 Hinault special Diamant and opted for a third bike which was as yet unknown but apparently only five or so years old. Neil was nervous but my assurances about it being Belgium and there being more bikes than people calmed him down somewhat.

'Bikes are loaned and shared there all the time,' I said, lying. 'And sometimes you have to borrow the best to be the best.'

We were picked up at the station and driven to the house. We made our way up the long driveway and there it was, leaning proudly against a tree.

A ladies bike. Touché Belgians.

I should clarify. By ladies bike I don't mean a pink one with streamers coming from the handlebars and flowers on the saddle. It was a ladies bike none the less, with its shorter top tube, stem and handlebars as well as a larger saddle. The colour, in a darkish purple was also tending towards the ladies side of bicycle paint schemes.

'There it is.' I stated the obvious and pointed.

'Macman. No.' He started laughing and dropped his bag.

'What do you mean, 'no'?'

'Surely this can't be for me, it's a women's bike isn't it?'

The other two bikes were still in the garage.

'Well, we can try one of those if you like.'

We spent the next three hours doing what Neil does best after buying: tweaking. He had bought a saddle and pedals to swap over so all we had to do was choose the bike. We managed to snap a stubborn saddle bolt on the Merckx and scratch the paint at the same time. This helped convince us that it wasn't a collector's item after all so we shouldn't feel too bad. Additionally it helped us decide it wasn't the bike for Neil. The Diamant went a similar way due to immovable and incompatible components which left us both realising the inevitable. Neil would be tackling the Flemish lions on a ladies bike.

Changing the saddle and pedals was a breeze on the more modern Ridley but Neil still managed to say the 'pony' word approximately twenty times during the process. We went for a test ride, with me on the Felt, and from my perspective it was finally nice to be riding with someone who had a worse bike than mine. After a few minutes he started to ease into a nice rhythm and was managing thirty-five kilometres per hour without growing breasts or a ponytail. I won't say that Neil was pleased, or Nellie as I was calling him, but an air of calm had descended. Perhaps the five hour trip to Belgium for a ride on someone else's ladies bike was not going to be a disaster after all.

'It's not too bad, though I am going to have to tweak the saddle, naturally.'

'Excellent. I told them you British were tough.'

'Just how flat is it here? Unbelievable. How about we put a new best ever top speed on this ten year-old bike eh? Here and now.'

Neil started clicking through the gears, rose from the saddle, and in close to the first cycling cliché of the book, put the hammer down. Aside from looking impressive his effort was effective and I struggled to keep up initially. Neil found another gear and moved his gloved fingers to the handlebars to get into a more aerodynamic position. I was forced to follow suit and tucked in behind him. The rubber band connecting us started to stretch out and I was taking in a few deep breaths. An intersection with traffic appeared in the distance and Neil eased off. I drew alongside him.

'Nice one. How does it feel?'

'Pretty good actually. Not sure how I will go for one hundred and sixty kilometres or so but I have to say it felt good. I think we are going to smash them, Macman.'

The British bulldog arrogance was back. He had hammered the Flemish ladies bicycle. Next up was the Flemish seniors bicycle team.

We returned home after the short thirty kilometre ride and bumped into Lucien in the kitchen. I introduced him to Neil and we told him that the bike was fine and we were ready.

That evening we tucked in to a massive bowl of traditional Flemish spaghetti bolognese followed by a few pots of chocolate mousse.

Neil knocked back the opportunity to have a Belgian beer over our meal. Incredible. My father-in-law must have been nervous watching this demonstration of dedication and professionalism but he hid it well and instead reached for Neil's share of the beer.

RACE DAY
(Chris)

Race day was finally here. The first of the Belgian attack cyclists arrived at eight am, right on schedule. He was a short, hard-looking man, and there was no mistaking that he worked the land. He was brown from the sun with bright blue eyes and deep creases across his face and looked like he had just stepped out of a spaghetti western. The others followed soon after and were all clearly from the same cantina. A lifetime of tough living, tougher farming and long riding stared at me like the sun and I turned away humbly toward my shoes. As each shook my hand their wide eyes stared in concentration and they barked a few welcoming words in English. Men vs. boys didn't quite describe the marked difference between us.

A man called Lud was last on the scene. He was introduced and then walked back out to his bike to retrieve something forgotten. I noticed that each of his calf muscles was like a leg of ham. If it was a cartoon I would have gulped loudly.

Meanwhile Neil was still getting ready, applying the finishing touches, zippering and shining and straightening and stretching somewhere in the back room.

We were playing up to the stereotype of being over-dressed, over-pampered and over-here. Neil met Lucien earlier and we had laughed while he made himself fried egg sandwiches for the ride. Lucien laughed equally as hard in return when we lined up our bulging packets of gel, beetroot powder, power bars and eye of newt. He shook his head while we counted out what we would need every forty-five minutes according to empirical cycling evidence.

Neil suddenly appeared in the doorway. The eyes of the room swung toward him. There he was, the Greek god of cycling. Black Assos SS Mille jersey. Black Assos Campainissimo bib shorts. Oakley Polarized Radarlock Path sunglasses in white. White Sidi Ergo3 Carbon Vernice shoes. I was in awe of the complete cycling vision before me. I swear I heard a clap of thunder and the opening guitar riff from *Bad to the Bone*. There had to have been a sliver of fear in the Flemish hearts though these stern faces betrayed nothing. There was only silence. Neil Wiggins was here, sans mutton chops, and he was going to ride.

Neil broke the tension with a timid hello and a wave and looked down shyly at the astonishing athletic reflection bouncing off his sparkling shoes.

There were introductions. Ludo, de Lud, Lus, Ludy and Marcel. At least that's what it sounded like with the 'R' in their Dutch being rolled and hence similar to the 'L'. Ludy may have been Rudy.

The eldest of the Belgians, who would have been in his late sixties nodded at Neil.

'I tink he looks like he's going to be going very fast.'

Belgians can't make a 'th' sound. Not one.

'I wouldn't know about that. Looks can be very deceiving.' Neil responded with good grace and well-practised English reserve, playing down his ridiculously superior legs and ability.

'Go easy on us eh? I am just an old man.' He laughed and his shoulders shook.

'Come on. I think you should go easy on us.'

Well done, Neil. Keep it up.

It was true though. While we were furiously adding kilometres to the legs in recent months the Belgians would have been preparing the same way they had been for years which is just to eat fries and cake continuously, drink beer and do four hour rides every couple of days. Their groundwork had been finished years go. Come rain, hail or shine (mostly rain as it was Belgium after all) since they were in primary school these Flemish knew how to belt out a chronic all day rhythm on a bike. And here they were, getting ready to show those English speaking gringos how it's done.

We reached for gloves and helmets. I chatted to Neil briefly. I heard Lucien explain to his mates in Flemish that we had gels, powders, bars and all the latest fancy-pants equipment. There was nodding and laughing and shaking of heads, and looking back now I think I can say there was disdain.

We said goodbyes to wives and daughters and made last minute checks of the brakes and wheels for no good reason.

I noticed Marcel had only one small bottle of water on his bike. The other bottle cage had a spare dusty tube stuffed inside it. So he was planning to ride one hundred kilometres on half a litre of water like some sort of camel. I pointed it out to Neil and he shook his head.

'Hey, Marcel. Don't you like water?' I asked.

'What? Oh, the water.' He looked at my two 750ml bottles filled with water and sports drink mixed with Neil's magic dust and he smiled.

Clearly they weren't taking this seriously enough.

Neil climbed on the ladies bike with a sigh. While the Belgians were mounting their carbon stallions there he was dressed to kill riding a fairground pony.

I tried to cheer him up.

'At least no-one knows you around here.'

Seconds later we were out on the road. The shape of the peloton for the day was established in seconds. There were Belgians in front, Belgians in the middle, and an Australian and a Briton at the rear. I looked at Neil and noticed he was busy adjusting his gloves. We stretched our backs, shook out the legs muscles, turned our necks from side to side like idiots and prepared for the longest ride ever by anyone on earth, almost.

We were laughing when we took off. I was delirious. I had a whole day to spend on my bike, in the company of other cyclists, real cyclists from Belgium, and I was also going on a long ride with my mate Neil for the first time. The first few kilometres were bliss. Each pedal stroke was velvety smooth and with the early start there was zero traffic so the only sound was the faint reassuring whir from our chains. The whole day stretched in front of us gloriously. The conditions were perfect, cool and dry. Although we were expecting breezy conditions later there wasn't a puff of wind around the departure point amongst the farmlands of Essen.

The road at the start was as silky as the pedal strokes and we covered the opening few kilometres at around thirty two kilometres per hour. I then realised my first mistake for the day. I forgot to tell Neil there were cobbles.

Cobbles cannot really be described to a non-cyclist. They sound quaint. Nice even. They remind one of historic town squares, church steeples and the charming old-world. To a cyclist however, cobbles are bone rattling and bike breaking. The cobbles are worn through daily use by tractors and trucks and are uneven, bumpy and spread out across the road rather than stacked neatly side-by-side. Many cobbled roads in Belgium, and especially the ones in the north near my father-in-law, look as though they have been dropped from a plane like a cobble duster. The gaps between each stone can range greatly and there is no safe line to follow. Some of them are half overturned.

In the great annual Paris Roubaix one day classic race, known as the Hell of The North due to the location near World War I battles there are sections ranging from a few hundred metres to three kilometres but never more. It is the most prestigious one day race in the world, but many pro riders refuse to race the event believing it a circus event where they are the clowns paid to perform. Riders crash regularly, knees are dislocated and seasons ended. Roadside support teams change between twenty and fifty wheels per race. The winner receives a mounted pave stone and holds it above his head in victory if his skinny and tired arms will allow.

When riding on cobbles your whole bike vibrates violently, bouncing you up and down and shaking you from side to side. The teeth jar, if you can feel them, and you are convinced from the clanging and banging that your bike will break up due to its re-entering of the atmosphere. Advice from pros is to ride in a big gear, as quickly as possible, to keep pressure on your back wheel, and to keep your hands soft on top of the handlebars rather than gripping them.

Cobbles are particularly arduous for people built like Neil such as teenage girls and Alberto Contador. The heavier pro cyclists like Tom Boonen and Fabien Cancellara and me, for instance, can push hard and grind through the pave. The cruel truth is that the faster you go the easier it is and the less you get bounced around.

Worse was that we had Belgians in front of us. The Belgians naturally love cobbles. Of the last five Paris Roubaix events, four have been won by Belgians. They call the cobble stones kinder koppen, or 'kid's heads'. This is either because the shape is like that of a child's head or because they just want to snuggle up to the little darlings and keep them lovingly warm and safe and away from foreigners.

I warned Neil.

'Blunners, I forgot to mention. There's ummm, there's going to be a few sections of cobbles'

'What?'

'Pave. Stones. Cobbles. You know.'

'Where?' He managed to lace a one word sentence with dread.

'Two minutes from here, max.'

He swore.

'And then, maybe a few minutes after that.'

He swore again then asked; 'What do I do? You didn't tell me this, Macman.'

We were both laughing, though my laughter was perhaps a little louder and longer than his.

'Put more tape on the handlebar maybe. That's what they say.'

'It's a little late for that now.'

'I think we are supposed to ride as fast as we can. And don't hang onto your handlebars too tightly otherwise you will be peeling your fingers off later. Let's stick to their line I guess, maybe the middle of the road, where the tractor wheels don't go. I guess. Maybe. Don't you watch Eurosport? You should know.'

My mixed message would have given him no comfort.

Neil added that he needed a wee.

As we came up to the cobbles I noticed my father-in-law turn around. Was that also a smirk there on his lips, visible at fifty yards?

The sudden clanging and juddering noises from the Belgians in front indicated they were on the pave. I had a massive grin on my face when I reached the first stone. Here we go.

The grin soon turned to grimace as we shuddered along and the stony surface sent violet vibrations through bike and body. My watch band popped open. I swore loudly. The watch dangled loosely on my wrist and I made a V with my arm and wrist at the apex to stop the watch from rocking toward the handlebars. Meanwhile the laughter and swearing coming behind from Neil seemed to grow eerily distant. I turned my head around briefly and saw that he had slipped off the back of our group by two or three metres.

Dropped in the first few kilometres, with one hundred and seventy to go. Oh dear. Blunners. The combination of cobbles and laughter had slowed him down substantially; especially given we had only just begun the pave. A car thundered loudly past the group. I began concentrating on pushing the legs hard and keeping the hands soft, as well as stopping the laughter. I looked around again and saw Neil had fallen a few more metres behind. I really had to crane my neck around to see him. He was definitely off and out the back. At this point I worried for him a little. His confidence would have been as shaken up as the rest of him. I slowed down a touch so that he could rejoin.

By now we young athletes were a good five metres behind our sixty-year-old Belgian cycling friends and slipping further. At that point at least they weren't aware of our slight hiccup. Looking to the front though I noticed one of the heads dart around to see where we were. It was Lud the calves. One head soon became all five heads looking at us. Great. Now we were being talked about. One Nil to the Belgians. I raised a 'thumbs up' signal to them. All ok. Nothing to see here, fellas.

We soon adjusted and managed to hang on and the gap stayed at about twenty metres. My watch continued to swing nervously around my wrist. I didn't dare take my hand off the handlebars to snap the clasp back. At one point I found a gutter to roll into away from the cobbles but a pedestrian soon sent me darting back to the wicked stones.

We made it through the cobbles after another few minutes. It took five minutes all up to cover only two and a half kilometres of pave on a dead flat road with no wind. Not good. At least the new road felt like a putting green.

Neil rolled up alongside me.

'Bloody hell, Macman. I couldn't stop laughing,' Neil said as he reached down to tighten a shoe strap.

'I know. My watched band popped open.'

'I can't believe they're already in front.'

'Don't worry. There's hours to go. We will get them back.'

'How many more of those do we have to do?'

Neil raised himself out of the saddle and pushed off, with me following. We quickly caught them and settled back down. My father-in-law asked me how it was going.

'Gaat het, Chris?'

'Ja. Alles perfect.' I lied. He knew.

I looked at Neil to wink at him but he was looking away fiddling with something on his jersey. We were in the same formation as before with Belgians in front, an Australian in the middle, and a Briton at the back adjusting and making sure of the one per-centers.

We were averaging thirty to thirty-two kilometres per hour which was more than manageable at the rear of the group. There were long stretches of empty roads, with no sound at all aside from our chains. We passed through a similarly quiet village in Huybergen with its lines of poplars, and headed toward Hoogerheide.

Every time I looked at Neil he was adjusting, eating or taking one of his ten sips of sports drink per hour. The attention to detail was dazzling.

We began preparations for our turn at the front of the group. Averaging thirty-two kilometres per hour in front was fine for a few kilometres but when it was our turn we had it in mind to increase this, ever so slightly, and to stay in front for as long as possible. We wanted to make absolutely sure we never dropped below their average speed, by hook or by crook. The best time to move up of course would be when the wind was stronger and forcing the group to slow, or when we were in an open area with miles and miles of straight empty road in front us. We didn't know where we were going so navigating through a village centre with instructions being called out to us in Dutch from behind would be tiresome.

The guys in front dropped back and were replaced by Lud the calves and Marcel. We were in the second row now, ready to make the move. We were in Holland, and on the most incredibly smooth bike paths, made of perfectly flattened bitumen. The temperature was twenty-three degrees and only the occasional cloud marked a blue and sunny European sky. There was still little by way of cars or hills and only a modest breath of wind about. It was a cyclist's paradise. The kilometres ticked over at a rate higher than I was used to. We were on flat terrain and in a group and we had passed through only one traffic light in the first hour.

'When are we on, Macman?' Neil asked.

I noted the riders in front were swapping over after every ten kilometres or so and it would be our turn soon. I asked Lucien when it would be best for us to get 'op kop'. He told me there was a path along one of the canals which would be perfect, and it was a few kilometres away.

I reported back to Neil who smiled and told me to 'take the Hog gel.'

I reached around and fumbled though the gels stuffed into my rear pockets. I found one of these special spikes of warm blackcurrant-flavoured sugar jelly that Neil was referring to and swallowed it down like a nasty overgrown oyster. I twisted my head to help force it through.

Fifteen minutes later we were alongside the canal and Lucien turned to indicate it was showtime.

'Righto Blunners. We're up.'

'I need a wee.'

We rode to the front. Neil was out of his saddle.

Lud winked at me as we sped past. Another Belgian yelled out to: 'take it easy on the old men eh?'

It didn't take long for things to go awry. I looked down at the clock. We were getting carried away. Thirty-five kilometres per hour. This was higher than Neil's magic number when he trains; evens, as in twenty miles per hour. Neil edged his wheel slightly forward of mine.

I ignored the speed for the moment though because I was finally riding in front of the Belgians and loving it, the flag bearer in a cavalry charge. I felt a bit more at home up front and into the wind as I always train alone. Sitting at the back, although physically easier, had less appeal. I suspect Neil was feeling the same way hence the youthful over-exuberance on both our parts.

I looked at Neil. 'Should we slow down?'

'What for?'

'Dad's army behind us.'

'I'm on a girl's bike. I embarrassed my country on the cobbles. These guys are Belgian, they'll be fine.'

We looked at each other and then turned to look behind in unison. Our sunglasses, Mad Max black outfits and dead pan expressions must have been intimidating though to their credit the Belgians hid their fear well.

We stuck to this new high speed effort for about ten minutes. Neil's front wheel stayed about one inch forward of mine throughout. It was a massive show of determination and defiance. He was the leader.

Then the Belgians blew up. By blow up I don't mean in the cycling sense as in dropping out of the group but in the Anglo-Saxon sense of getting upset. Something must have sparked them off because they all cried out simultaneously:

'Hey. Come on.'

'Slower please young 'uns.'

'Remember we've got a long way to go.'

'Beetje rustig altsublieft. Zeg mannekes toch.'

We apologised and settled back down to thirty kilometers per hour. Neil smiled at me and winked.

The new score was one apiece. We peeled off toward the back of the peloton and told each other how good we were.

My father-in-law said that we were soon going to stop for a quick break. The group had ridden seventy five kilometres in just over two and a half hours. At this stage I still felt good and was hoping to reach the magic one hundred kilometre point before having a break but a few minutes off the stiff bike saddle sounded promising.

Pulling into a beautiful old Dutch town, Zierikzee, we rode slowly along the cobbled streets and crossed a bridge through the gates of the walled city before stopping at a cafe; De Gekroonde Suikerbiet, or The Crowned Sugar Beet.

Neil ran to the bathroom for his long awaited wee. He had done marvelously to last this long and said so himself as he walked awkwardly off across the stones of the street in clipless cycling shoes with full bladder.

In the meantime sandwiches of all description including the famous fried egg were scoffed within seconds and washed down with cokes, coffees and powdered drink.

Minutes later the helmets returned to sweaty heads and we continued on.

The next ten or so kilometres were fine. Then the rot set in. Neil and I began comparing notes on how each other felt, perhaps testing the waters for signs of fatigue. I asked Neil what was happening with his usual niggles and his knee. Neil kindly asked after my shoulder and back, and asked whether I thought it might flare up. Neil told me he was a cycling pharmacy and could give me anything I wanted if I had any pain or inflammation. His pockets were full.

Eavesdropping on the Belgians I only heard chatter of crops, what so-and-so was doing and the weather.

Some gentle whining between Neil and I started at about the hundred kilometre mark. We were into our fourth hour on the bike and it was beginning to show. I wondered aloud whether training for more than two hours a week would have been better preparation. Neil told me this would only have made things worse and would have provided opportunity for more injury.

'The less you train the less chance you have of hurting yourself while training,' he said.

Meanwhile the Belgians continued to cycle in their carefree way, laughing and looking around at the beautiful Dutch countryside and ladies.

As we reached the foot of the Zeelandbrug (or Zeeland Bridge), the gates began to go down forcing us to stop. Blessed relief. We took some photos of the five kilometre long bridge and one or two of ourselves looking splendidly athletic. As the ships passed and the gates opened it was agreed that Neil and I would go in front again.

We were also told we could go a little faster here and naturally we didn't resist. Like a pair of idiots we took off like rockets again in front of the Belgians. I was first out of the blocks and ahead of Neil and looked down to see we were passing forty five kilometres per hour. Once again Neil was laughing and yelling out to all: 'Oh look, he's on the drops!' (the drop handlebars).

At the other side of the bridge we were told to slow down again by the Belgians. There was more tut-tutting. This was fine as the lungs were now heaving. We settled back in to the thirty kilometre average speed for a short while.

From the one hundred and twenty kilometres mark Neil and I began to moan to each other in earnest, at least every five minutes or so. There was no major complaint, but the difference this time was that we were discussing our own niggles and pains rather than inquiring about each other. My back was beginning to ache. His knee was starting to stir.

The last twenty kilometres were altogether different. They were shocking in fact. Neil and I flipped between laughing and groaning in equal measures. My whole body was sore. My butt cheeks were dead from the saddle and throbbed with pain. My shoulders were shot. The hands hurt. How could the hands hurt? I think it was from gripping the handlebar for five hours. No amount of shifting around or trying out any new position seemed to help. Neil said his shoulders were fine but his neck hurt, and he had cramp in his calves. We were swearing profusely and had more than enough of the bikes.

The Belgians on the other hand had been eating up the miles with nary a care in the world. They were happily singing and chirping and whistling away, taking turns in the lead, counting clouds and merrily talking to each other and to passers by. All the while their legs had been grinding away at this thirty kilometre per hour march onward without faltering or fading or showing any signs of fatigue. They were like clockwork. A constant, relentless and unvarying group working together, and we were beaten.

'Mate I'm burying the bike when we get back,' Neil said, 'in the backyard. I swear. Owww my knees are killing me.'

'Look at these blokes they're like animals. I'm in awe. It's a disgrace.' I wiped my face. The lips were dry and disgusting.

'I know. They are just machines. Have to say I wouldn't mind seeing how they go in the mountains though. It's this constant flat that gets me.' Not all of the bulldog spirit had left Neil's beaten body.

'Yeah that's true. It's the monotonous, level, incessant ride that makes it hard, right? They would be hopeless anywhere else, or in any other sport. What can Belgians do apart from cycling anyway? I took my father-in-law out in the surf at Manly. Not with my board or anything, just in a few feet of waves. You should have seen him. No idea.' Now I was being pathetic. I let out a little delirious laugh and swore.

'Yeah these guys are crap. We could smash them.' Neil said to more feverish laughter.

It didn't end there. We had doubled back on ourselves and were making our way close to home which meant one thing. Cobbles. The stones were as unforgiving now as they were six hours earlier but our fatigue made them easier somehow. Maybe we knew what to expect. Even my watch couldn't be bothered unfastening itself. Neil and I only had each other to beat now and worked hard at staying with the Belgians over those horrible cobbles. A few minutes later we pulled into De Bostella cafe. The ride was over.

We drank a few beers in this cafe back in Essen and played up to our sorry state. Play-acting was unnecessary of course as our physical appearance, slumped shoulders and deathly slow movements off the bike painted a clear picture. Sitting out the front of the cafe in the sun we raised a glass together to Belgian cycling prowess with a 'Chapeau' and pledged to get back to training. After a few beers we waved goodbye, gingerly clipped into our bikes and rode home alone, promising to come back with better legs next year once we had dug our bikes back out of their resting place.

We didn't turn around again. I am sure if I had I would have seen five Belgians staring in our direction and wetting themselves with laughter. They had seen off the Australian and the Briton in a canter. Easy, like shelling mussels. No final score was awarded. I would have settled for two-one, but they had probably put three or four past us.

Walking through the door in Essen I could tell by the laughter of Wendy and mother-in-law that we looked like the walking dead. A combination of one hundred and eighty kilometres and three beers had rendered us both speechless. We barely managed a scattering of chuckles and a few shakes of the head all evening.

Later that night I mumbled something to Neil about re-thinking our plan to do this type of ride in France, unassisted, for twenty one days straight, with mountain climbs. Neil started laughing and agreed.

'No chance. No more bike for me,' he said.

DUDE LOOKS LIKE A LADY
(Neil)

When Chris asked if I would like to go for a ride in Belgium with his father-in-law I felt instant euphoria at the thought of cycling on the continent, with continentals. These weren't just any continentals either but the passionate people of Flanders who hold cycling up in it's rightful place as the number one sport bar none. I had sat glued to the Belgian classic races in April every year without fail, often wondering if I was the only person watching across the whole of Britain. I couldn't wait. Though a fan of Belgians and cycling, I doubt Chris truly understood the magnitude of what this meant.

Once this euphoria subsided however I had to look into the logistics of travelling away from my young family to Belgium for a weekend. I needed to take time off work too, and had to explain to my wife that my leave allowance would only be chipped away by one measly day. I would make it up to her and get around to doing some chores on the to-do list. However, the more I looked into it, the more it sounded like a pain in the neck.

Chris wasn't very helpful. He was replying from the comfort of being the man already in Belgium and thought that it would be a very simple process for me to make my way across the channel. 'No worries' he wrote in that languid Australian accent of his, over email. He would even go out of his way to meet me at the station.

I love my bicycles and initially thought it best that I dismantle the most precious of these before packing, transporting and then re-assembling on arrival but the thought of four hours of bike building, aligning and tweaking for only a six hour ride sent me soft.

There were three modes of transport available: ferry, train and plane. Ferry and plane were quickly dismissed due to cost so the only real possibility was to take the Eurostar to Antwerp. Again this seemed a very simple process but in reality bikes and English transport aren't all that compatible. I read a few horror stories about broken forks and bent wheels and started to get cold feet at the whole idea.

Chris didn't understand. He spoke grandly of the cycle-friendly Belgian rail network where I would be treated like a long lost son and where my bike would probably get a better seat than me. He assured me that my bike and I would be well looked after. He completely ignored the part about having to travel through Britain first. Email is a wonderful tool for selective response and Chris is a great exponent.

I eventually asked Chris if he could look into hiring a bike and this time he threw himself into the task. He trawled Belgium for race bikes for hire. E-mails were sent, queries dispatched and calls made. Everything seemed to come up blank until out of the blue I had an email from Chris' father-in-law asking what size frame I would need and how tall I was. Chris said that as the big man of Belgian cycling was now involved everything was going to be ok.

The trouble was I had no idea what size frame I would need. My own bikes were size 'small', which wasn't entirely helpful. I estimated my frame size would be a 52-53cm from friend's bikes I had ridden in the past.

In the meantime I booked the train and started the usual preparation of buying new kit and cycling weapons of mass ingestion.

To Chris' father-in-law though my body dimensions signalled a few warning signs and he confided in Chris with his worries.

'His body is longer than his legs. Are you sure you got the details right?'

Chris said he would check again and thought I was perhaps joking. I wasn't though. I had been punished in the legs department, being at least a couple of inches shorter than what they should have been given my height. After much searching, the Belgians finally managed to find a few bikes suitable for someone with stumps.

Chris sent me an e-mail with pictures of the bikes. I gingerly clicked on the attachment secretly hoping for a classic Colnago or Merckx. When the first picture opened I was presented with a circa 1960's bike with downtube shifters and quill stem in a frightening shade of green and white.

Nice one, Macman, you had me fooled there. I quickly clicked on the next picture to be presented with a Merckx, not just any

Merckx but a flat barred Merckx. It was a good looking bike but something didn't seem quite right.

It took me a while for my brain to process the image until I slowly but surely realised that the frame looked as if it had been designed and built for a child. It was far too late to organise any other mode of transport now however so I packed my mountains of expensive gear and 'preparation' ready for the trials ahead and hoped for the best with the bike.

I should add I was slightly concerned about transporting the preparation through customs. There were powders, gels, juices and pills and as I was journeying alone I didn't have anyone else with me that I could frame. I was most nervous about transporting the notorious gel apparently endorsed by the one and only Johan Bruyneel. The 'Hog gel' as it became known took on an almost mythical status during our e-mail exchanges. Would we take it before the ride and blow those Belgian pretenders away with a turbo charged performance or would we save it till the end just to give the old blokes a chance before we took an historic stage win?

British customs let me through without question and I soon found myself on the way to Antwerp.

Chris and his wife and daughter gave me a warm and friendly welcome at the station. I hadn't actually seen him in person since my work stag night about seven years earlier but he didn't seem to have changed that much.

I was staying at the home of his in-laws. When I arrived I was enthusiastically welcomed but there was no sign of the legendary Lucien. I didn't know what to expect but the majority of sixty year olds back in the United Kingdom appear on borrowed time busily getting ready for the big sleep cycle. Chris had told me to expect a skinny hairy Belgian.

Whilst Lucien was away we had the chance to look at the antique machinery on offer. The two bikes in the garage both seemed to have fundamental issues. When I sat on the Merckx the top tube was so short that the handlebars were almost touching my knees. I decided to move the saddle back as far as it would go. I tried the bolt with an allen key and it just wouldn't budge. A liberal spraying of Belgian lubricant seemed to have the desired effect and the bolt creaked into action before promptly snapping off in my hand. Damn. Chris was mucking around with his bike across the garage.

'Er, Macman, I started off with one bit...... now I have two.'

'Better hide it for now. Maybe we can replace it tomorrow.'

I moved onto the next bike, the green and white Diamant something or other whilst kicking the evidence of bike vandalism out of view. Once astride the Diamant my position felt pretty good. It was time to attach the pedals and take it for a ride. I'm not sure if grease is actually used in Belgium because yet again trying to move the original equipment was an absolute bugger. After liberally spraying half a can of Belgian lube on the offending pedals they finally came loose.

We set off and immediately and my very expensive and perfectly white Sidi cycling shoes began rubbing against the cranks......ahhh. This was not a big issue in the scheme of things and nowhere near as dangerous as the trouble I was having changing gears on the pre 1950 downtube shifters. However, I felt like a learner driver shifting gears in a car, looking down at every change which led to a swerve whenever I shifted gear.

I suddenly hit a bump and felt the whole front assembly move an inch and then wobble back into position. Added to this when I pulled on the brakes the mild deceleration was so imperceptible I thought about packing a drag chute.

Meanwhile Chris was rocketing around on his new, but very cheap Felt, and dropped back to ask me how the bike was.

'Er yeah, not bad thanks.'

What a whopper.

We rode back to the house and I genuinely began to panic at the thought of riding an antique for six hours on unfamiliar roads while elderly Belgium riders scrutinised the foreign devil's every move. It was going to be interesting; especially as Chris' previous insistence that he was hopeless on the bike was appearing a shade false. I had hoped to at least keep *him* in check.

When we arrived back at the house Lucien was waiting. How can I describe Lucien? For starters, the man (man is the only way to describe this specimen) was sporting the kind of tan Hollywood film stars pay thousands to possess. I didn't know they had sun in Belgium. This guy must have used the lot. He had the look of a gentle Bjarne Riis, quizzical, powerful and lean, and possibly with enhanced cyclist's oxygen-rich and thickened blood.

He looked me up and down, I was paranoid and was sure he was calculating whether or not I would take my turn at the front as hard and fast as a Flemish lad or barely hang on to his illustrious band of geriatrics.

Lucien soon put me at ease and greeted me with, quite obviously, a vice-like gorilla handshake. I saw those hairy arms for the first time. He asked in broken English how the bikes were going and then left us to it.

At this point in time I had done all I could to avoid the elephant in the room, or the lady bike against the tree as it were. This third option was staring at me the whole time but I just couldn't do it. I gave it a derisory glance a couple of times while turning bolts and playing with other bikes and had noticed that apart from the short top tube and bar shifters it looked a good bike.

There was just one tiny problem with it of course. It was a *girl's* bike. I didn't want to wear a dress to be the best. How could I? No, no, no. The more I thought about it though the more I realised I had no other choice. After all, we had trashed one bike and the other was going to wear holes in my three hundred pound sterling shoes.

To his credit, Chris only laughed for five or so minutes after I said it was going to have to be ladies day after all. The next two hours were spent tweaking the she-bike before we settled down to some spaghetti. At least the Belgians knew how to carbo fuel.

Much like the Etape I couldn't sleep well the night before this big ride either. I was pumped. Like any good cyclist I turned to pharmaceutical assistance and swallowed a sleeping aid.

In the morning I walked downstairs to a table creaking with the weight of food. No-one knows how to do a continental breakfast like the continentals. There were loaves of bread in a diverse range of colours and styles as well as ham, salami, cheese, juice, mountains of hot coffee, the lot.

Lucien was busy frying what seemed to be a carton of eggs at the cooker. Chris had warned me of Lucien's fried egg sandwich fetish which was his staple diet on the road. Lucien is extremely low tech when it comes to cycling nutrition. His pre-cycle meal looked like it was taken out of a 1968 edition of Eddy Merckx's Big Book of Cycling.

I opened up my bag and gel upon gel spilled out onto the table. I could feel Lucien's frown on our scientific approach. He would be cycling on 'pain et de l'eau' and maybe a tiny but thoroughly denied dollop of EPO.

The Belgians started arriving from around eight onwards and unsurprisingly these old guys looked very fit. I was dressed in my Assos shorts and top and even though I looked the part I felt out of my depth. Chris decided that this would be a good time to start winding the Flemish up with some commentary on Australian and English riding talent and suggested they take pens and paper in jersey pockets for some note taking.

It was all weather beaten faces, granite calves and huge quads. The big Australian words fell on deaf ears.

We were ready to go. I moved to my bike and realised I hadn't checked the tyres. Lucien took one look at them and waved me away.

'They are fine.' Think Darth Vader.

I daren't argue.

We set off slowly onto the main road and I sat myself at the back of my new peloton which probably had the combined mileage of to the moon and back in their legs.

After a few kilometres we met a slight head wind and I put some increased effort into the ride. The bike started clicking in and out of gears. No matter what I tried I just couldn't get a big gear going. Chris was laughing and joking with the Belgians in pigeon Flemish, telling them what he was going to do to them and I was at the rear, beginning to wonder about the next 159 kilometres. I adjusted the cleats on my shoes and now they too began causing some problems. My left calf started twitching...uh oh...the excuses were coming. I had to pretend that everything was fine.

We went through a section of cobbles which Chris had conveniently forgotten to warn me about. This was far and away the worst five minutes of my cycling career. I dropped off the back by a couple of metres from the sheer shock of it and pretended something had come loose to hide the sorry effort.

Chris was still chatting to the Flemish and cruising up and down the group like it was no effort. I was bolt upright on my girl's hybrid and the wind was really telling. I looked over. Was Mac suffering? Maybe a slight curl of the lip. We had only covered ten kilometres or so, but we had set off a bit too fast.

Soon we were into a rhythm though and I stopped my internal whingeing long enough to enjoy the ride and marvel at the thought of being out on the road in Belgium for a whole day.

At about the fifty kilometre mark it was our turn at the front. We had been joking for months now about a combined Australian-British show of supreme strength and wound ourselves into a frenzy. We started pushing thirty-five kilometres per hour and higher, into a strong wind. My lungs were contracting deeper and deeper and my calf was twitching badly but this was our turn to shine.

I smiled at Chris. 'This is easy mate. The Flems are on the rack.'

'You got it mate.' He struggled to reply, with faltering breath.

One by one the Belgians began to fall silent. The pace was having an effect on the locals too, time to turn the screw.

I turned back to the road, locked into my own private torture. I felt sure that Mac was in the same boat as me. It was too late now though. We couldn't slacken the pace or get off the front without appearing like complete jokers. On and on we went along the coastline, wind crashing into us. Then suddenly we seemed to be moving further inland. Oh joy, the wind calmed somewhat.

A short time later a junction appeared. I had no idea which way to go but there was also no way I was going to spend one minute longer suffering on the front. This happened to coincide with some shouting behind us so I slowed to a halt. The red puffing camels then came to the front and took the reins, with a slight but obvious downward turn of pace.

One of the Belgians, the one with the biggest calves rode alongside me.

'You er, how I say, you put the hammer down no?!'

I generously laughed along with him. I had no idea if he was being serious or not.

'Petite.' I replied. Not sure why or what I was trying to say.

'You ride a girl's bike?'

'Ha ha, yes.' I replied through gritted teeth.

'I bet you have a beautiful bike back home.'

At around the seventy kilometre mark we pulled into a picturesque village and stopped outside a pub. We commandeered a table outside and ordered litres of coke and water.

Lucien and his pals shifted nervously in their chairs whilst suspiciously looking up and down the road. Then when everything was deemed safe each rider subtly took out a large silver foil wrapper from their rear pocket. Lucien delicately un-wrapped his package with loving care whilst I sat there astounded that he would even contemplate this in public.

Nothing was going to stop him as he took the package contents in both hands and raised them to reveal something I still struggle to write…. a fried egg sandwich on white bread, coated with butter. He had no shame. How was he ever going to be the best when he ate the worst? I decided then and there to buy him a subscription to a Men's Health magazine by way of a thank you, if such a thing exists in Flemish.

The lunch stop was the last bright spot of the day. The Flemish riders soon resumed their positions at the front and ground away at a speed which equated to torture. It was the Flemish Inquisition.

With their metronomic pace never raising or lowering despite changes in terrain and wind and time the Belgians hammered us. As the day wore on Chris and I grew silent aside from the odd moan and I even detected a slight grumble from Chris as I swerved in front of him during one particularly low point.

We only had one more turn at the front and foolishly tried again to put the hurt on. Of course, we only ended up hurting ourselves. The last fifty kilometres were a fight to stick with the group and a fight against the pain in my calves, neck and back.

I must have looked at the kilometre count on my bike at least once a minute for the last two hours. It took every ounce of energy to turn the pedals and steer in a straight line and even the gentlest of inclines saw my eyes rolling to the sky. At one point we had ridden down through a farm near a train crossing and had to ride back up through a humble climb of no more than fifty metres but the effort to simply hang on was extraordinary. I was an absolute wreck, the only thing that made me feel better was looking at Chris who had a face like he was giving birth.

We were shot. They killed us. We stumbled into the pub once it was all over and spent five minutes folding ourselves into the chairs like geriatrics. We put on a pair of brave faces and bought the Belgians a few beers. We joked around with them and encouraged their mocking at our expense. At least you could say we were good losers.

The last thing I said to Chris when I waved him off at the station was that civilians won't understand what we have been though. As

I sat in the carriage on the way home I cursed the continent and cycling in general. It was time to hang up the cleats.

MID-LIFE CYCLING
(Chris)

On the return to Hong Kong my thoughts about becoming a giant of the road in France were unchanged. Neil's 'no chance' was spot on. At least we had no chance of doing it while our kids were young and while retirement was still twenty years away. The Belgians had given us a glimpse of our sixty year-old selves however and showed that with twenty years of cycling and farming we could develop the mental and physical fortitude required for such a monumental feat. Twenty years of cycling would naturally be fine but the farming was going to be difficult to come by. Maybe I could lift A4 paper bales in the office instead of hay bales to get in shape.

The mid-life cycling therefore continued in earnest and I was happily back on the as-yet-unburied bike. Being free of the grip that the tour dream once had around me meant I could enjoy riding for riding's sake. I still kept a tally of the distances ridden but this was for fun and for a sense of achievement rather than to hit a set target for the week. I even started night riding.

I retained the sense of guilt when leaving the house for a ride. I'm not quite sure when this will ever go away and I'm glad that Neil shares the feeling. From talking to other cyclists I know there are some who relish the prospect of leaving home for a ride as much as I do, but they additionally stress that this is their right and their time, and cycling is part of the package which their families understand. Hence they are wholly free of guilt and cannot fathom my weakness in this regard.

Wendy understands and accepts my need to exercise the legs for a few hours every week but when it comes to my daughter, Milly, my self reproach weighs heavily. I always slink off with my head bent low. When we lived in Australia it was a bit easier. Milly was younger and I could put her in bed for a nap, duck out for a surf and be home two hours later. When I walked back in the door she would still be asleep or only just waking up. From the age of three when the naps stopped, the guilt started.

Weekends are 'Daddy Days' and we talk about plans for the upcoming weekend from about the Wednesday or Thursday. Daddy needs to be there on Daddy Days. Often I will prepare her during the week by letting her know that I will be away on Saturday morning for a couple of hours.

In order to assuage the guilt I leave as early as possible or late at night when my daughter is in bed. That way I don't have to look at any trembling lower lips or hang-dog expressions as I slip out. Forget a sparrow's fart it is more like a night owl's fart when I leave the house. Most weekends I like to be out at around five am.

Preparation begins the night before. We don't have a maid so the bike gets to rest permanently in the spare bedroom. For the early morning rides the bike will come down from its perch and the tyres will be pumped. The brakes are checked, as are the lights, both front and rear. The small pouch attached to the saddle is checked for the bare minimum of tools and tubes and it is strapped tightly.

Next is the kit. Jersey is decided based on weather and my performance the week before. If I had a poor ride and was overtaken by De Rosa or anyone else equally annoying then a different jersey would be selected. I would hate any passers-by to think they nailed the same rider twice. Maybe the Belgian club jersey would come out. If I rode well however then the same jersey, since washed, would be laid out on the breakfast table in readiness. Black bib shorts are placed alongside the jersey. There is no rain jacket. I own a couple but we don't do those in Hong Kong. The chances are that, yes, it will rain at some point during the ride but it will be hot enough to make you live with a wet jersey rather than sweat it out in the jacket.

Food is also arranged. This is always a fad thing. One minute I could be addicted to gel, especially the espresso variety. The next week it might be power bars. Various types of power bars are appetizing and remind me of space food sticks from primary school but these demand bovine chewing capabilities and can take fifteen minutes to get down the throat.

Recently the old school Belgian waffles took over. These are easy to chew even with a dry mouth and they taste fine but are essentially cobblestones made of flour, sugar and fat. I bought a dozen recently and had one per week until they ran out. I suspect it is the last packet I will buy until 2020.

Finally then the bidons are smelt to determine whether they are acceptably clean. If unsoiled and dirt free they are then filled with water and stuck in the cages. A waterproof plastic bag is also dug out from a kitchen drawer and cash, phone and bus card are placed inside.

Done. Ready to go.

The alarm is set for four thirty which will have me out of the house and on the bike twenty to thirty minutes later. A three hour ride means I am home at eight, with eighty-five kilometres under the belt.

This new routine saw me settle into a pattern of around one hundred and eighty to two hundred kilometres per week, all on the road and either late at night or in one of the five o'clock starts in the morning. On afternoons when my daughter was invited to a birthday party, I used these opportunities for a daylight cycle around Discovery Bay.

The average speed improved with almost every ride and my weight dropped about five kilograms from the Belgian trip. Unfortunately this weight came off my face as well as my belly which gave me an altogether tired appearance like many cyclists of forty, but I was obviously prepared to sacrifice good looks for good legs.

Around this time I also received a visit from a training partner in Hong Kong in the form of Lucien. As we know, he cannot go cold turkey for more than a few days without a ride, so we agreed to tackle some roads the day after his arrival. He was going to ride my mountain bike, with me alongside on a road bike, so we would need a lumpy route with a few hills.

It was my first ride outside Discovery Bay. Logistics came first. In order to leave the area cyclists need to ride to the bus stop and take the airport bus through a tunnel connecting the suburb with the outside world and the airport. Bikes are stored in the luggage section underneath. Sounds easy.

We leisurely drifted down to the plaza to board the airport bus. There was plenty of time to spare before departure. I was standing on the pedals, looking around, shaking the legs out and taking it nice and easy. At the bus stop however I noticed the sign: 'Bike riders must use the last stop before the North Tunnel'. Suddenly we had only minutes to get to the other side of Discovery Bay which is about three kilometres and includes a decent hill.

We made it with a few seconds to spare. I was sweating by the time we arrived and Lucien was showing signs of heaving lungs. I wasn't the only thing dripping either. When I retrieved the bike from the luggage compartment on the other side of the tunnel, a massive two minutes later, the contents of my bidon had emptied onto a fine piece of Louis Vuitton carry-on luggage destined for the airport. The bus took off before I had time to re-board and apologize unfortunately.

We planned to do an easy route around Lantau island with a reasonably steep hill in the middle. On the other side of the tunnel another cyclist, in full BMC kit with BMC bike, gave us the full rundown. He explained that the little hill I had chosen from a map was in fact 'a killer'. I laughed and said the hill was sounding more like a mountain.

'Correct, you might have heard of it,' he said, 'it's called the Beast of Tung Chung.'

I had in fact heard of it at a party a few weeks earlier when a fit-looking Kiwi triathlete told me about a beast of a climb he had completed in Tung Chung where he was forced to zig and zag across the road diagonally to manage the gradient rather than go straight up.

Mr. BMC looked at our bikes and noted that Lucien certainly had enough gears with his triple set but hesitated with my bike and said I would 'enjoy the challenge'.

There was no way of backing out of the beast. In fact it sounded like fun and a good opportunity to demonstrate to Lucien I had matured as a rider.

So off we went, trailing behind Mr. BMC who soon became run BMC as we let him lead us out on to the foot of the climb. Killer hill was right, as was Beast. Run BMC started bouncing up and down on his pedals and was immediately out of his saddle. I clicked through to the last of my gears and had a horrible feeling they would be woefully inadequate.

Lucien sat behind me. He seemed to be trying to keep a few gears up his sleeve as I heard him change at least twice in the first five hundred metres even though the gradient remained constant.

The road crossed back and forth above us, so for the few moments when my head wasn't looking down at my wheels I could see the climb rise steeply to the left and then rise equally to the right and there was no end in sight of the switchbacks. I wasn't even sure how long the hill was so couldn't motivate myself with thoughts of being close to the finish.

Every cyclist's companion, the imaginary man with the hammer, visited with about one kilometre of the hill to go and never left my shoulder. At this time I looked around and noticed that someone else had recently left my shoulder. Lucien's chain had come off. It must have been that one last gear change.

I didn't want to look behind to see whether it was just the chain or something worse. I couldn't afford to lose momentum or, horror of horrors, get off the bike in the middle of a climb. The slope was close to twenty percent. Not good. I knew that he had been in Hong Kong for only one day and I couldn't just take off and leave him there. I stopped. I turned and saw he was about fifty metres further down the road. I yelled out to him, breathing heavily and grabbing desperately needed oxygen into the lungs.

He yelled back that his ketting, or chain, was off. After a few minutes he waved and re-mounted the bike and started up again.

By the time he had ridden up and past me he was laughing, with a very red face, and I had my breath back and felt better. Unfortunately I found it close to impossible to get my cleats in the pedals on the hill and had to use the old trick of riding sideways to the gradient to clip in, while also laughing, and avoiding the Chinese buses coming in either direction.

Once we reached the top I can say there was much heavy breathing, little by the way of chat, a modicum of swearing, and some desperate guzzling of the last mouthful of drink that hadn't splashed onto the Louis Vuitton.

I agreed with myself that I would take this Tung Chung beast on again.

RONDE VAN VLAANDEREN
(Chris)

Eventually, after a few months had passed, thoughts and discussions with Neil returned to the Tour, and there was a brief dialogue about completing the course together in 2014. Memories of boastful Belgians and broken spirits had faded and been replaced by new legs from regular training in Kent and Hong Kong.

Realistically, though, we both had the work questions to deal with. Getting a month away in terms of time and being able to switch off mentally from work issues was going to be a little difficult. Aside from this we still had young families. While the kids and wives still wanted us around it was not fair to leave for a month, nor did we want to. Neil also had a newborn to consider. Furthermore there appeared to be a backlash of sorts in the media against middle-aged office workers pathetically championing their last sorry strands of remaining youth by attempting a desperate, monumental physical achievement while hitting up friends and family into the bargain by demanding money for charity. Additionally, we didn't have the guts.

We ran through a number of different options along the same theme of becoming giants of the road but with fewer kilometres. It was going to be more David than Goliath. One idea was to ride the French Alps in a week. Nope, couldn't do a week away. Paris-Roubaix, a ride of around two hundred and sixty kilometres in one day, was also tabled but then quickly stopped due to cobbles, logistics and costs. Starting the ride at the designated departure point on the outskirts of Paris amongst overturned cars and Molotov cocktails without assistance from the gendarmes was also an obstacle to consider.

Neil was going to have a weekend away so it had to be close to Kent. What about Belgium? Bingo. Why hadn't we thought of that before? In the end we decided that we would ride the longest route ever for either of us, at two hundred kilometres plus, around Flanders, and most importantly, unassisted. I guess in one sense the last piece could be considered a non-compete clause. Perhaps we did not want the ride spoilt by sixty year old Belgian machines. Or from another viewpoint maybe with our new lungs and leg capacity we would hurt them and be forced to slow down and nurse them through. It's possible.

The route for our own Ronde Van Vlaanderen or Tour of Flanders was cobbled together using Neil's brand new GPS. Although I use the word cobbled I knew that there was no chance Neil would select a route with any trace of an actual cobble, stone, pebble except in the town square of Bruges which was the planned midway point. The plan was to start at Amerikalei in the centre of Antwerp and then head in a north westerly direction before lunching in Bruges and returning home and all the while avoiding major thoroughfares.

We ran the route past Lucien. This friendly request for advice was an olive branch looking for guidance and a blessing from the great man of Flemish cycling as well as seeking fresh ideas and asking for any concerns to note. Had we, for instance, selected a route which included busy roads or dangerous levels of traffic? Would we see the beauty of Belgium in all its glory from the vantage of a bicycle saddle where it is best enjoyed after all? Or would we be riding through refineries, gas works, coal mines and broken towns?

Lucien sniffed across email that 'the route is fine'. In those four words it was obvious he resented the lack of invitation. There was clear disappointment that we weren't asking him along to give us another cycling lesson. We hadn't afforded him the opportunity to assert his power and dominance and constrict us between his hundred thousand kilometre thighs. Again. I think on the contrary he should have been happy we spared him the embarrassment of being beaten on his own green Belgian turf. That would have hurt more than not being there. More fool him.

What we didn't realize is that we were going to pay for this snub. That good ole Belgian cunning was ever present in Lucien's 'the route is fine'. It wasn't fine of course, and we were going to suffer for it. More fool me.

Two weeks out from the Ronde Van Vlaanderen Neil began preparing the way he knew best. It was that same precise preparation he has employed since turning novice in 1998. He bought new kit. Neil says that this groundwork is the way to get the legs ready, the heart right, the blood pumping, the lungs at max capacity and, of course, the head in the zone.

Again Neil decided that we should be Freds in Black, so he bought himself a top of the range jet black Molteni jersey and insisted I follow suit and make that same sixty pound purchase. Excellent.

In the final week before the Belgium ride the training tapered off. For Neil that meant no more internet browsing for bags, saddles, cleats, gloves and glasses. It also meant even less time on the bike than the forty minutes he did the week before. Neil said that he needed to wind down the clock and let the legs lie low. A bit of him time was due, he said.

Neil was bringing the carbon Boardman bike with him this time as he was making the journey by car. I say car but I mean Subaru Impreza WRX. On arrival Neil told me he received the 'thumbs up' signal from a number of Belgian motorists and I am going to leave it there. We unpacked the beast and I showed him the bike room in our house. Neil picked up one of his seven or eight suitcases and tipped out a sea of gels, creams, bars, potions, powders and lotions.

The cycling paraphernalia was an impressive beginning but then he trumped that with a neat peal of his Levi 501s to show me a sparkling white and utterly hairless ladies leg. Neil had done the big shave. I should surely chronicle my shame here at having half-agreed with Neil to whittle down my own legs before chickening out. I never completely agreed though, and in the days leading up to the shave-down I had backed down. I had also told him I was not going to do it. I wasn't man enough, or was too much of a man. Additionally my wife said on twenty occasions she finds shaved men's legs disturbing. Although comments like this have often encouraged me to do the opposite, on this one I think she had a point. Neil, if we do Le Tour I will do Le Shave.

Neil was proud of his legs and I was slightly envious. He explained that if I was to do it eventually I should consider myself well informed there will be a lot of hair. He repeated 'a lot' and said it 'will be a very messy and nasty business'.

We once again ate a mound of traditional Belgian spaghetti bolognese on the evening of the big event and indulged in only a couple of Belgian beers. The alarms were set for six am. We planned to be out at six thirty and to complete two hundred and ten kilometres at an average of between twenty-eight and thirty kilometres per hour. It should have been easy for two giants.

Alarms were unnecessary because I was awake at five and desperate to get out on the bike. Neil had stayed in Milly's bed while she slept between me and my wife. Unsurprisingly, he hadn't slept well. With his superb well-honed Contador-like cycling physique he told me that this lack of rest was a mere trifle. Once again the professionalism was bursting through

Neil's complete focus was also in evidence at the breakfast. We were sitting there in our cycling kit like tightly wound athletes, ready to pounce on a day-long cycling feast. I fuelled up Australian style, on a serve of nine slices of white bread slathered in honey, butter or vegemite as well as an apple Danish and a Belgian custard-filled koffiekoek. I couldn't get enough of the stuff. I wanted to just grab a bag of flour, pour water on it and knock it down, with butter. Two mugs of coffee sealed it. Neil was a picture of calm and poise however and had a slow petit dejeuner of one banana, one slice of toast and one glass of water. Even at the dawn of this epic journey, Neil refused to allow one calorie more than necessary into the Blundell bag of bones machine. Chapeau.

'Don't you want something else to eat, mate?' I said between mouthfuls, 'what happened to carb loading?'

'Oh, go on then.' He agreed and grimaced his way through one more slice of bread. I am going to stage an eating disorder intervention on Neil one day.

Final preparations were made and we walked slowly downstairs to the bikes. There should have been a song playing in the background like Eye of the Tiger. Milly rushed over to help out. I had been telling her about our 'bike race' for months. Often back in Hong Kong while I was perched on the trainer in front of a pro-cycling race on television, she would sit watching with me and ask if I was going to do the same thing. Unsurprisingly I answered 'yes'. In theory I was. I would be riding a bike a long way in Belgium, in full cycling kit. It wasn't much of a lie, really. So on the big day she was as excited as me and was up at six, running around the house, passing around gels and filling water bottles. As we wheeled our bikes out through the hallway my daughter pushed her way past us in her pyjamas, opening the front door to the deserted city of Antwerp at dawn.

She looked up and down the street.

'But Daddy, where are all the people?'

'What people, Honey?'

'Where is the crowd? Where are all the people on the side of the road?'

She was disappointed that her mid-life cyclist dad was not as well supported by the fans as she had seen on television up Alpe d'Huez.

With a kiss and a wave and a click into the pedals we were off. We crossed over Amerikalei and ducked through the well cobbled streets of fashionable Antwerpen Zuid district towards the river Schelde. We made it to the river in minutes without passing a soul and streaked along the riverbank via a rather fruity pink bike path. Moments later we pulled up at our first stop and waited for the lift down into the Voetgangers (pedestrian) or Sint-Anna tunnel which took us under the river and west of Antwerp. The tunnel was built in 1933 and is thirty metres below sea level. Being at just over five hundred metres long it meant one of our allotted two hundred and ten kilometres of Belgium was going to be in an underground tunnel.

No matter, we were soon out from the impressively smooth bunker and onto the open road at Zwijndrecht. Six months of planning, training and buying unnecessary kit was about to be put to the test. Neil looked down at the device mounted on the front of his bike and with gloved finger started pressing a few buttons.

'Let's hope this thing works eh? According to this we need to do down that road there,' he said.

Neil had plotted a course into the gadget which would take us from one side of Belgium to the other and back. When we emerged from the tunnel there were only two roads to choose from. Neil pointed in the general direction of one with some confidence and we marched on. Excellent. The wonders of modern technology. I was quite jealous of this computer which would not only tell Neil where to go but also tell him his heartbeat, cadence, speed, wind direction and all sorts of mileage information. Less important in Belgium but still nifty none the less, the device also displays the gradient of the road and height above sea level. In our case it was going to veer between zero and zero. All in all, it was going to be a vast improvement on dismounting every few kilometres to unfold a map.

After a long straight stretch of a few kilometres the road split in two, close to Melsele. Neil once again confidently pointed in the right direction. He was able to look down at the machine's display with ease, even in the low lit dawn and whilst wearing impossibly cool and equally expensive sunglasses. We were travelling at a nice speed and warming up for what would be a long day.

We sped through small town centres and villages at an average of thirty kilometres per hour in the first hour or so. As the sun began to slowly peep through early morning clouds we found ourselves seeing less and less of the villages, and more of the farms, with beautiful green spaces opening up. Neil was only intermittently looking down at his modern mobile map for assistance as we made fast work of the first few sections.

Then came the first warning. Neil shouted at me from behind.

'Mac, stop.'

I freewheeled for about fifty metres and slowed to a halt. I turned and saw Neil standing with one leg on either side of his bike. His hands were cupped around the screen of his device.

'I think we've come the wrong way. I can't see the training bike icon which is supposed to be just in front of us on the map. Hang on, it's saying we should be over there somewhere.'

He nodded toward an old farmhouse.

'OK. Should we try that?'

We re-mounted and rode back toward the previous intersection.

Moments later we had set off down the new path when it happened again.

'Mac, stop, blimey.' He assumed the position again, one foot on either side of the bike with hands around the device.

'Same again? But there are only two roads we could have taken,' I said.

'I know. Maybe it's… I can't see with the glare... hang on.'

The sun was out and shining on Belgium now.

'So it's saying… Oh I see what it's done, it's started making a new route toward Bruges because we were going the wrong way. It comes up with a suggested way, you see? But because we turned around and are going the way we should have been originally, it is now saying we are going the wrong way. So it should re-adjust again.'

I stood staring silently at him.

'Yep that's what it's done. Let's try that. Sorry mate this is pony. Geez, hopefully that will be the last stop.'

'Don't be sorry mate, you are the guy stuck looking at the map every two minutes while riding at our dangerously high speeds. I'm just freeloading.'

I felt bad. I should have made more effort instead of relying on a device I couldn't afford and couldn't use.

That wasn't the last stop. The next fifty kilometres descended to farce, with poor Neil driving us on hard in one direction and then skidding to a stop minutes later. Our average speed slowed dramatically and was dropping further with every delay. At one point, according to the thoroughly detailed information we were able to dissect weeks later, we had a stop of eight minutes while we stood staring at, and shielding the sun from, a screen the size of a business card.

Where oh where were the map-free cyclists from Essen? Only they could have helped us now. How rude of them not to come.

We bought some water at a shop close to Assenede and agreed that we needed to shun technology and go old school. At times previously when we were going in the right direction we noted where the sun was. We decided now that if we continued on with the sun in a vaguely similar part of the sky we would find a way to Bruges. There were also bound to be road signs.

This method was also fraught, as every twenty kilometres or so we would end up on the central motorway, or an offshoot. This meant more doubling back, more looking at the sun, more looking at the device's compass application and growing frustration.

We eventually made it to the town centre of Bruges two hours behind schedule. I asked Neil what our average speed was and I cannot bring myself to write it down, even now. I don't know that I ever will.

We found a cheap restaurant full of tourists in the town square and did our best to hide sweaty and grimy faces, gloves and helmets. In spite of the variable riding we had still covered one hundred and twenty kilometres in the saddle so there was hunger to be sated. I ate a margarita pizza in about five minutes. To my great shock Neil did too. This was not a good thing though as it was an indication of lost repose. He was flustered and had forgotten the calorie intake of the average tourist pizza. Four large cokes and two litres of water rinsed out the dry throats.

We took exactly nil pictures of Bruges, that photogenic Euro paradise, and instead took off east away from the sun toward home. We had work to do.

On the outskirts of Bruges I went into a newsagent and bought a large foldable map of the Antwerpen province and stuffed it into a jersey pocket. If Neil's thousand dollar compass could get within range of Antwerp we could have the ride licked.

The ride home was much like the ride out, a stop start affair of around twenty U-turns, a slow to moderate average speed and a healthy application of swearing. From kilometre one hundred and twenty to one hundred and eighty there was a lot of laughter though as we realised how funny the situation was and how stupid we looked to the cars which honked and beeped at us, and to the drivers who wound down windows to tell us to get off various motorways. Naturally, the Belgian rains also arrived and helped to darken moods that needed no further darkening. At one abrupt dead end, flush up against the main freeway, we rode left for one kilometre looking for the way out, then right for one kilometre, then back on ourselves for one kilometre, then realised there was a cycling bridge over the freeway which had been staring at us the whole time. In the rain. For fifteen minutes.

The map disintegrated due to the downpour and we were soon back looking for signposts to Antwerp. The lowest point of the afternoon was the water stop in a little town called Middle Belgium. I can't remember the name to be honest. The town was deserted; the square, the main street, the back streets and two parks were all devoid of people. It was three o'clock in the afternoon but it may as well have been three in the morning. In hindsight we should have bought water at the last town but didn't see a shop and wanted to make good time. Soon though we were desperately parched and so once again began a five kilometre per hour crawl.

I saw a tiny spot of light peep behind the curtains of a shop in the distance which looked like a newsagent and we rode over. I was wet, tired, red-faced, helmeted and ugly looking and I wasn't sure whether the shop was open so gingerly pushed at the door. To my surprise it opened and I saw a till in the corner where the light was coming from, and a small queue of people. Ahhh, there were inhabitants in the town after all.

I found four bottles of water on the dusty floor in front of shelves of soup and queued for my turn. There was a lady in front of me clutching car keys and a cigarette lighter, she was probably buying cigarettes. In front of her was a gentleman checking his lotto results. He had three folders full of tickets, possibly for other family members also trying to win. There was a red folder, a green folder and a yellow folder. The lady behind the till fed each ticket into a machine. If the ticket won then a little jingle sounded from the register to the tune of 'I'm in the Money'. He would then buy new tickets with the modest proceeds and run those back through the machine to check the results. If 'I'm in the Money' played again, he repeated the process. And so on. And so on, until all of the tickets in all of the folders were exhausted.

A pool of water had formed under my feet where I stood dripping for those nine minutes. A dam of frustration also welled up inside me but I managed to keep it in check and retain the outward appearance of a pleasant, happy tourist.

I did not explain any part of the episode to Neil when I emerged from the news cave after ten long minutes and he didn't ask. No words were spoken. Instead we guzzled down one bottle, filled our empty bidons with the rest and rode off.

One bright spot requiring observation was our fitness. There was never any mention of a bad back, sore shoulders or slit wrists. Naturally we were fatigued from having ridden on a bicycle saddle for nine hours but all of our training and jersey buying had paid off.

We arrived back in Antwerp at around five in the evening, having ridden two hundred and thirty kilometres. This was twenty more than we planned and reaffirmed our status as Giants of the Road. We had completed what we set out to do which was to take on a massive ride together and have a laugh on a bike. The images I have from that day still bring a smile.

Back home, Milly ran to the door and gave me a huge hug and a kiss and looked up and down the street again, wondering where the crowds were. She asked if I had won.

'Yes of course.' Luckily Neil was out of ear shot.

'But Daddy, where are your flowers?'

On returning to Hong Kong, Wendy took up daily walking as a way of keeping her blood and energy flowing. She says it is not power walking, but she wears athletic attire and makes a marked effort with her stride so perhaps intensive strolling is closer to the mark. She told me the other day of an incident where a pregnant lady, who was perhaps in power walking mode, had the temerity to overtake her. Wendy said that in response she then put her own foot down, passed the pregnant lady and powered off into the distance.

I remarked that it seemed a lot similar to the stories I had told her of my own refusal to accept being passed by cyclists. I said she had mocked me for this type of behaviour. Wendy responded that it was altogether different. It wasn't a male ego issue like mine; rather, if a pregnant lady was able to walk at a certain pace then my wife should be able to keep up with her. I agreed with her. This made perfect sense and it was crazy of me to think otherwise.

Neil sent me a mail one day after our arrival in Hong Kong. He suggested we start a new training programme and complete Le Tour in 2014.

ON-LINE REDLINE
(Neil)

I take a sharp left at breakneck speed, carrying as much momentum through the corner as I dare. I carefully avoid the loose stones and pot holes in my path. My heart skips a beat as I feel the instant hit of adrenaline in my veins.

I straighten the bike and quickly rise from the saddle, hands firmly grip the drops. I brace myself as I begin to hammer the pedals. The gradient starts to bite and my fluidity begins to falter slightly.

It is still early on the climb so I concentrate on bringing my cadence back up. Any redundant weight has to be jettisoned. I throw my bidon to the side of the road and briefly watch as it only just misses a dozing squirrel. I will pick it up later.

I change up a gear. A new more intense pain is now pounding in my thighs as they quickly fill with lactic acid. I try to increase my pace still further, digging deep inside. I use a combination of upper body strength and legs to keep my progress as smooth as possible but now my breaths are coming quickly and erratically.

The gradient flattens slightly and I use the opportunity to sit down and spin my pedals. An internal argument reigns fiercely inside.

'This hurts, slow down.'

'No, it is the same for everyone, let's put the hurt on.'

I know the flatter sections should not be used for resting but for gaining more speed so I leap out of the saddle once more, change gear again and accelerate up the road. The back wheel begins to creak and flex under the effort (I tell myself) and the brake pads momentarily touch the rims.

My mind is now foggy and vision is restricted to the road directly in front. I need more oxygen, or better still another lung or two.

The 'summit' eventually comes into view and I use this sight to push every last ounce of energy I have left into a sprint. I finish the climb and before the fatigue slowly takes hold of my entire body I just manage to push the stop button on the bike's computer. I free-wheel down the other side.

My head hangs low as I try to come out of my oxygen debt, my nose drips onto my bike frame and I wipe my face. A violent hacking cough breaks the morning silence.

I glance down at the time split.

Two minutes and thirty five seconds.

Fifteen seconds outside the best time.

I hate you Peter Quinn.

I had recently changed my whole approach to cycling. I bought an application for my phone which meant I could target specific climbs in the area and ride them as fast as possible, recording the exact start and finish times. Hundreds of other local cyclists also use the application and in effect provide a virtual competition and leader-board. Having thrown the towel in on club rides, night rides, morning rides, long rides and weekend mountain climbs I decided I needed something fresh and this device was going to give me a new lease on cycling life. I planned to be the King of Kent Mountains, or at least, king of the hills dotted around my town.

It was a blessing in one sense as it helped chart my progression on a series of timed sections and it showed that I was in reasonable shape compared to other cyclists. Mostly, however, it was a curse.

The first time I checked a route I had just ridden, I did not expect miracles. I was just out enjoying the scenery, spinning the legs and getting some fresh air and decided to stupidly upload the ride to see how it all worked. I also wanted to check the distance and elevation. The device was dead simple to use and displayed the route alongside a series of timed sections.

Wow. There were a few of my times displayed as second fastest recorded, amazing, and even a best time, I was obviously going faster than I thought.

I clicked on the 'overall' link expecting to see my name shining brightly at the top of the virtual leader board only to be presented with someone else's name. Peter Quinn.

Where had my fastest time gone?

It then dawned on me that it was *my* fastest time, which apparently was only thirty-sixth fastest overall. As I had covered the same section a couple of times the results were compared. So first and second was against myself only. When lined up against the locals I was thirty-sixth.

Out of forty.

A few emotions occurred at this point. Disappointment and embarrassment seem to reign supreme though. How could this happen? I don't deserve this public humiliation. I had used my real name too when instead I should have called myself *Big Dog 52* or something equally clever.

I stared at the screen in shock when the second jolt hit.

The Maillot Jaune beat me by forty seconds, on a two minute climb.

How is this even possible? Am I that unfit?

Denial took hold.

I thought he must have been cheating, either by positioning the device in a moving vehicle or by hitching a Cav-style lift on the wing mirror, or more likely by taking large quantities of Belgium's finest EPO.

Slowly, denial turned into a sharp realisation that yes, the times were right and yes, I really am that bad.

Exploring the local area, I strove to find a few hills that were close to each other so I could see if going full bore made any difference to my status.

For me this was the kind of riding that I hadn't tried for years and certainly not since I turned into a mid-life cyclist.

I was too used to tapping out a relatively low pace for an hour and a half once a week. This type of attack riding required an altogether different approach and one that needed change if I was going to bag myself a mythical KOM, King of the Mountain.

Rather than go out and train immediately, I instead set about buying kit and tweaking my bike. A lower more aerodynamic position on the bike was essential and would require some minor tinkering. I decided to lower my stem. I attempted this simple adjustment in the garden at about eight thirty in the evening.

Undoing the bolts and slipping the stem off, I suddenly heard a sharp twang. I desperately fought a losing battle to tighten the headset up but it was too late, the expander plug had fallen through to the fork.

I took the whole thing apart, tipped it upside down and found the missing plug. By now the light was fading fast.

Laura returned from her run and I got her to hold the bike whilst I put it all back together.

I then tightened it all up only to discover that the fork now wobbled. Oh dear.

Yet again the bike was stripped down, pieces flying all over the place and by then I was using a small flashlight. I decided to take all the pieces indoors and dragged it through the house, wondering whether there were still a few vital components left outside.

I dusted off my copy of the 'Big Blue Book of Cycle Maintenance' to give me some kind of a clue but a few flicks of the page didn't work either and the expander plug kept falling out.

I decided to fire up the laptop, desperately searching through the web for 'wobbly fork'.

I spent the next ten minutes in the garden with a flashlight looking under the tables and chairs, convinced that there must be a crucial part that I missed, but there was nothing.

After two more hours and considerable swearing the fork then actually fell out of the frame. I wondered if Chris had the number of his fabled Hong Kong bike shop bloke who might be able to talk me through a fork and frame re-assembly for a fiver.

I finally admitted defeat at eleven forty pm and went to bed knowing I had no choice but to take it to the local bike shop.

My local bike shop is called Wiggle and they can generally get me everything I need at a handy discount with a bag of Haribo chucked in for free. I needed mechanical help this time though, and it was time to get back to the shop in Rainham.

How was I going to explain the problem? In the past I had come up with some incredible tales for explaining away the various twisted bits of metal that I have manage to fashion under the heading of 'bike maintenance' with a shrug of the shoulders. Considering my ham-fisted attempts to fix this particular issue though I was concerned I had managed to do some permanent damage. Perhaps because I am older and wiser now I decided to tell the truth.

With this in mind I guiltily walked through the front door and was confronted with some beautiful looking bikes. I wondered whether I should just buy the best to look the best to be the best.

I met Simon, a friendly guy who said he would take a look at it for me. I mentioned I had to pop out but would be back shortly and he said that it was no problem. When I eventually returned, after a receiving a rather nifty haircut, my bike was out the back and evidently all in order.

Simon told me the bike was fixed in a few minutes and wouldn't cost me a bean. I could have hugged him. I didn't even ask what he had done and to this day marvel that this bloke could repair in less than five minutes what took me five hours to ruin.

No matter, with my new and improved aerodynamic position on the bike I was sure to shave off at least one or two seconds per ride. It is the one-percenters after all.

I told Chris of my plan to become King of the Mountains and suggested he do the same. Unfortunately for Chris though the hills around his part of Hong Kong were all around three kilometres long or more, very steep and take at least ten minutes each, even for a top cyclist. He is also built solidly like Spartacus rather than Schleck and would find the going tough.

I planned to bag a tiddler first and take it from there. To aim big, I needed to start small.

As I only had around an hour a week to ride I had to find a KOM within twenty minutes of my house. As luck would have it a number of very minor uncategorised 'climbs' were within a stone's throw of my house.

I donned my extremely expensive cycling gear and set off at the usual time of six am to set about making history. I was taking on Munns Lane in my first official KOM ride.

The precipitous five percent gradient and hellish three hundred and fifty metre length meant business. There was only way to take on a monument like this. Big ring, full chat.

Turning onto the hill I stamped on the pedals and looked very much like the late great Marco Pantani as I flew to the top. Admittedly the last thirty metres or so were fairly painful but I had set a marker. I then rode onto the next hill, the even shorter Hollow lane, and had a pop at that.

Once home I was engulfed by my daughter who was asking where I had been as she had missed me. Ahhh. In full cycling regalia I sat down to feed my son and chat with my daughter over her morning toast. I had managed that tricky combination of family time and winning a polka dot jersey before breakfast. A few minutes later I discretely pulled out the laptop, without the kids noticing, and uploaded the ride.

I was speechless.

I was KOM on both Munns Lane *and* Hollow Lane.

Admittedly if you added my times on both climbs together, it came to a mighty sixty one seconds but I was now firmly on the map. Forget thirty-sixth out of forty I was now Numero Uno.

Over the course of the next four weeks I pushed my body to the limit in a vain attempt at local greatness. Chris was enthused, asking for updates and checking the results but seemed reluctant to take on the challenge himself. Actually, he was less than reluctant; he had converted his weekly hundred kilometre rides to very brief sprint interval training and was riding even less than I was. Hibernation, I think he called it. After the trials of the year he needed to recharge the batteries and build himself up again for another season of mediocrity.

I continued in this fashion in the ensuing weeks and began to stamp my name on all of the leader-boards attempted. Riding in this style was extremely difficult as to even come close to a KOM I had to be pushing massive gears with massive efforts. Not only that but every climb had to be started full bore, on the rivet, with the big dog out and growling. It was also helpful to be carrying plenty of speed on the roads preceding the climb which lead to some fairly scary cornering on wet pot holed roads. But if I wanted to become the leader I had to take risks.

I should add though that this style of riding is frowned upon and is described in web and cycling circles as 'sniping'. Apparently a rider should concentrate on the whole long and laborious ride they are completing and then view timed sections from the perspective of the entire ride, rather than only attempt a one kilometre sprint.

After one month I grew into an expert on sniping and was reeling off one KOM per week. My time on the leader-board was always short-lived however as other snipers, and perhaps genuine cyclists, would soon supplant me by a few seconds or more.

I also found a new website which explained where I was going wrong. I could see that in the first couple of rides it was lucky I had come to a complete standstill at the side of the road immediately on completion of the timed section. On a few occasions, however, I had stopped metres short of the finish to quietly die and my time was therefore woefully short of the leaders. This new site also broke down each component of the ride and compared it to others in the leader board, allowing me to see where I was either losing or gaining time. It was a perfect tool for a sad mid-life cyclist with nothing better to do and I spent hours breaking down each ten seconds or so of the ride.

My statistics were familiar. I started off like I was being chased by Sweeney Todd on a quad bike then died a thousand deaths within twenty metres of the finish line. I soon developed a plan to keep a wisp of energy in reserve and push through the last few metres of each climb.

Week after week I trawled through the internet and pored over maps finding new hills to conquer. The results told the story. Stede Hill, KOM. Honeycrock Hill, KOM. Hartlip Hack, KOM. On a single day I managed two KOMs, a second and a third. I fired off an email to Chris with a link to my victories. Finally, I was once and for all laying claim to my position as an undisputed moderate cyclist.

It was not long before creaks started appearing in the defence however. The sniper became the sniped. Peter Quinn took back two of my KOMs only three days after I had stolen them from him. Then the Johnson brothers arrived and pushed me two places further down the list. I took it personally and bounced back to the top of the leader board on Stede Hill the following weekend. I then planned an assault on the Johnson brothers, preparing a route that could be ridden slowly until each KOM section where I would then lay down the law.

I realised I had lost the plot completely when the leader board became the first website I checked on waking up, before the news, or work, or anything fun. I had butterflies when the results were displayed and pumped the air if I was still the man on top. In short I had to grow up. I knew deep down I was pack fodder and unless I devoted every second of spare time to the sport I would never be a giant of old Kent roads.

Essentially I am a mid-life cyclist with only a few spare hours a week to get out onto the roads. These few hours will grow into half days and more in the coming years as the family matures and I look forward to some very long rides. I still plan to tackle Le Tour with Chris when I have a Belgian supply of kilometres or something else stored in my legs. Who knows when that will be? I just sent him a mail telling him to keep July 2014 free. In the meantime I will buy more kit.

ACKNOWLEDGEMENTS

Chris: Thanks to Wendy and Milly for the fun, the friendship, the family and the infinite patience shown as I tweak my bike and book. Big thanks to Mum and Dad for support and generosity through all my many years and for the little yellow BMX in Westleigh. Thanks Dave and Rich for accompanying me physically on these early rides and figuratively on later rides. Thanks to Brad and his red pen, our brutal first editor. Thanks also to Kate, Sandy, Will, Ash, Annabel, Tom, Will M, Sam, Gravox, Mik, Craigoss and Odgo. Thanks to Dave Van Ginderen and his attempts to get Boogerd on board. Thanks to Lucien for patiently teaching me the basics of cycling, and Suzanne for fuelling me for the rides. Thanks to Moray who is always able to tell me where I am going wrong, sometimes in a positive way, and whose friendship has enabled me to enjoy Hong Kong. Thanks to Tante Ria, the Kuystermans, the Wouters and their bakeries full of unbelievable goodies, and thanks to all of the Van Ginderens and Suykerbuyks for making me feel part Belgian and always welcome.

Neil: I would like to thank my Dad who for more than five years accompanied me on long Saturday and Sunday morning slogs in any weather, whilst dramatically falling off on a far too regular basis. He taught me, more than anyone, the true meaning of the word 'suffering'. Whilst I grumbled and moaned my way through fingers and toes so numb they wouldn't move, he stoically stayed silent and never once muttered a negative word. Even when his heart packed up in the middle of a ride. Chapeau.

Thanks Mum for washing the kit and the floor, carpet and chairs after I had created a swamp-like effect in the living room. Someday, I may forgive you for creating a hole in my beloved Assos jacket, but that time has not yet arrived.

I would also like to thank my wife and two children. My wife for accepting my feeble excuses when returning from my Sunday morning ride (yet again) rather later than originally anticipated. Yes, I never did get lost or have a puncture. I was busily adjusting the saddle height and angle, cleat alignment and bar tilt. I can't change. I am a serial tweaker.

To my children, Eve and James, I can only hope that it takes you longer than most to begin to read, and in doing so, delaying the truth that your father, despite his fantastic mountain conquering physique, is little more than a moderate second rate cyclist.

And finally, buying the right kit is more than simply walking into a shop and asking the rather bored spotty eighteen year old playing on their iphone directions for the Assos section. The right kit not only has to look good and have the best name, it also has to rate extremely highly in the cycling press. There is little point having bragging rights for owning the latest high priced kit if it has been panned in the cycling press as performing no better than a similar item from the budget bin. For this reason, I would like to personally thank Sidi, Assos, Gore and Castelli for ensuring that any mega expensive purchase will not only perform faultlessly, but will also comprehensively make me look the best, whilst I perform like a mildly asthmatic ant.

Het Einde

Printed in Great Britain
by Amazon.co.uk, Ltd.,
Marston Gate.